I'M **NOT** OK, THANKS FOR ASKING

F.E. Curtis, II

No, I do not weep at the world — I am too busy sharpening my oyster knife.

Zora Neale Hurston

© 2020 F.E. Curtis, II
All Rights Reserved.

Published in 2020 by F.E. Curtis, II and in partnership with Relentless Love, Inc. and CTK Strategies, LLC

Relentless Love, Inc.
8300 Greensboro Drive
L1-624
McLean, VA 22102
404-488-6571

All books by F.E. Curtis, II are available at bulk discounts for educational, professional and promotional use. If you are interested in bulk orders, please send an email to info@relentless.love.

Mr. Curtis is available for speaking engagements and, at the time of publication, handles all engagements, including virtual conferences, panels and lectures, podcast appearences, and in-person addresses of any kind via the informational department at Relentless Love, Inc.

www.relentless.love
info@relentless.love

Cover art work by Emily Neigel.
Illustrations by Briana Boykin.
Contributions from Yvette Pappoe, Latricia Wray, and Kelly Dawsey.

I put a sun in my lamp
I put a post-it note on my mirror
So I might love myself
So I might be enough today
I'm not OK, thanks for asking
I can tell I've said too much I'm out of touch
Guess no one ever really wants to know

Jamila Woods
Lonely, from her 2017 album HEAVN

CONTENTS

6 - You are Loved (playlist)
7 - I Love You to Infinity and Still Wonder, Why?
9 - A Nigger and a Midget
13 - An Ode to Marshall Mathers, with the express written consent of Black boys everywhere
17 - Manchild
21 - My Lawfully Wedded
24 - The Body
27 - This I Know

32 - A Rose is Still a Rose
35 - What If I Love My Wife Too Much?
40 - Windy
42 - A Moment in Paradise
44 - Positive Affirmations

47 - Maybe
49 - #MeToo
52 - Silhouettes Etched Across the Window Pane/The Orgasm Gap
54 - Woman
57 - Mississippi Love Letter
60 - This How I Feel When Sza's Prom Come on
65 - What Dat Mouf Do

69 - Bywater Blues
71 - The South Will Rise Again
74 - Black Men Don't Have the Luxury of Fearing Death

79 - Episodic
82 - One More Light (A Short Story)
101 - To the Lady at the Hippodrome Cafe that Used to Call Me Kendrick

107 - Ann,
110 - A Mother's Love
114 - Like Father, Like Son
116 - Depression Doesn't Win
121 - Summer 2020
125 - Alex Palace
128 - Birthday Thoughts/Forward
131 - An Open Letter to Eternity

"You Are Loved" Playlist

1) I Do This, Nipsey Hussle feat. Young Thug & Mozzy
2) Sandcastles, Beyoncé
3) Lonely Weekend, Kacey Musgraves
4) Wild Things, Alessia Cara
5) My Heart, Paramore
6) Always Remember Us This Way, Lady Gaga
7) Boulevard of Broken Dreams, Green Day
8) Ocean Views, Nipsey Hussle
9) So Loney, Jorja Smith
10) Last Hope, Paramore
11) Spotless Mind, Jhene Aiko
12) One More Lights, Linkin Park
13) Hey, I Won't Break Your Heart, Corinne Bailey Rae
14) 1-800-273-8255, Logic feat. Alessia Cara & Khalid
15) Grow Up, Paramore
16) Daydreaming, Paramore
17) Lonely, Jamila Woods feat. Lorine Chia
18) Satellite Call, Sara Bareilles
19) Static, Ari Lennox
20) Clean, Taylor Swift
21) Bad Idea, Cordae feat. Chance the Rapper
22) Don't Wish Me Well, Solange
23) Holy (Reprise), Jamila Woods
24) Double Up, Nipsey Hussle feat. Belly & Dom Kennedy
25) Born Tired, Jhene Aiko
26) LOVE, Jhene Aiko
27) Picture Me Rollin', Nipsey Hussle

I Love You to Infinity and Still Wonder, Why?

Rain Man[1]

Everyday.
I mourn.
    Cold.
Bloated caked face
In my favorite all-black Nikes

Wishing I was in the box
Pain searing deep
Down the marrow in my bones,
stirring like butterflies,
cacoons to evolutionary dragons

Evolution let me down, kinda mourn
God failed me and He hates me
Bullets fly and razors in steep supply
that kinda mourn

Malcontent, like running for the bus
and being in plain view of the driver,
only for 'em to press the gas

---

[1] Johnson, M. (Producer), & Levinson, B. (Director). (1988) Rain Man [Motion Picture]. United States: MGM/UA Communications Company

just as you was pulling out your pass,
kinda mourn

Perpetual.

Time serving as the axis of my existence,
spinning in its own haunting and wickledy
unexplainable distance,
indescribable and yet not healing so much
as a scar,
kinda mourn

Head rattled from the oceanic flow of tears,
top button still moist as the aroma
of soggy chicken fills my nostrils
yeah, that kinda mourn

Pits in ya stomach back at the slightest trigger
of sensibilities,
kinda mourn

Everyday, b.

I wonder what my brother could be.

A Nigger and a Midget

Caught Their Eyes, Jay-Z[2]

Coldplay in the background
Poster of the Queen from
Set it Off
Finally,
take the crown of a scorching
hot day, heat.
Mother greets.
I withdraw.

Heartaches fall through spring
Heals some come winter
I be wondering
OGs be talkin'
bout land of the livin'
how dat beats six feet under
and what not
I don't know, though
Not sure I can concur

Bells ring
And that sound don't dismiss you

---

[2] Jay-Z. "Caught Their Eyes." *4:44*, written by Jay-Z, No I.D. & Frank Ocean, Roc Nation, 2017.

Teacher do
Wish I could tell her
how much hate I got inside
Wish I could sit
in this room
Just a lil while longer
think of the homies that's no longer
And not visit the locker room
Not confront the outside world
Not have to be hard
Not have to pick a fight first because if I don't, he goin say somethin not the least bit clever, but everyone will say "oooooooo" and the lunch room or hallway will catch on
And then,
then I got two options —

    1. Punch a nigga dead in his nose
    2. Risk being the talk of the asphalt come time to hit the bus cause I was the roast of the day

And my parents don't play
but fuck that
I ain't bout to be the ass of no joke

I thought it ended, ya know
as folks got older
spose to get more mature
maybe had they balls drop
saggy titties, all that ish
But I was mistaken
turns out,

ignornace only multiply
and it's the same callous, soulless spirits
that'd be most fruitful and multiplying
And I'd be lying if I said as a kid
I ain't wanna end it

    I did.

But my desire for it all to be over wasn't a personal one
Not entirely
I made a list
Checked it twice
Circled names in red ink
Of all the kids that made me feel lesser than
Unprovoked
Unwarranted
The ones I never said anything to but felt the need to make me feel like I was lower than them because of the stature of my existence

"You're so confident in yourself."

    1. Shut the fuck up

    2. I ain't have no choice. I had to be. Everybody tried me, so I became slick with the hands and slick with the mouth at an incredibly young age. Come at me if you'd like. I'm a make sure you remember, forever, the day you came at this Titan.

    3. Y'all kill me. And some folks you literally kill. (Trans) And other folks you indirectly kill. (Suicide) You think it's a compliment, about how successful I am; how much I love myself; the extent to which I don't let the world define or knock me down; all

cause I ain't 6'3? What the fuck am I supposed to be? Should I quarrel into cowardness because your deep down inner being thinks I'm inferior because of the epitome of immutable? But y'all the same folks want an officer not to be scared of you cause you Black, right? You tweet three times a day bout how all Black women are perfect. Now representation matters? Now bullying needs to end?

   But I have discovered this principal in life – what goes up must come down
   And that's cool
   Bitterness never showed a fruitful harvest, and hate never eradicated seeds of despondency or despair. So I loved you through the pain, hard as it may have been. And now, now that we've discovered the eternal, that which is sacred and never holds His name in vein, know that I know who you really are. Know that I don't hold my breath, less the sea part, and even then my nostrils flow. Faith is the evidence of the unknown.

An Ode to Marshall Mathers, with the express written consent of Black boys everywhere

Soldier, Eminem[3]

"Don't ever try to judge me, dude"
    You don't know what the fuck I been through"

You don't know what it's like to hate your life
To be eight years old
holding knives
editing suicide notes
all while your "friends" sing Silent Night

When you born on a military base during another senseless war
When your father gets the call and thinks he's never coming home

When the asthma is horrific
Three years old, can't breathe
Ventilators losing their efficacy
Nothing else to do but pray on your knees
You don't know what it was like for people like me growing up

---

[3] Eminem and Luis Resto. "Soldier." *The Eminem Show, Interscope Records, Shady Records & Aftermath Entertainment*, 2002.

Ten years old,
writing notes bout who to kill
Knowing you were never for real
yet pleading
begging, crying for someone to care
Knowing that if this note don't get help
you'll be hanging yourself from the rod in your closet
With your dad's leather belt

But you struggle with kicking out the chair
out of some twisted, sadistic despair
Cause maybe ending your life is better with a gunshot to the head
I mean,
hanging is less efficient and easier for cops and fire
They simply bring you down
    no dried up blood wandering
        thickening like jello for your family to cleanup
But then you kick the chair and you're left there

        kind of hopeless

            just kickin'

                with no xscape

                    until it's over

Pull the trigger and it's seamless
Tense, terse and relentless
But it's a scene your brother and sister would never get out their head

So you move to the bottle of pills by the side of your mother's bed
But you get curious bout how long it'll take to succumb to the overdose
how unbearable the churning might be until you finally cross the post

I swear
No one understand the depth of my senseless heartache
The pain I encounter each and every time I open my eyes
Reconciling the many moments when people that claim to love you
probably tell you the most lies

Don't ever try to judge me, girl
Don't call my phone asking when I'm getting married
Don't tell me it's about that time
Don't spend a millisecond counting my dimes

I'll tell you something
Let you in on a lil secret
See, I don't think nobody really care about me
I don't think no one really got my best interest at heart
Y'all don't really understand
You don't really know what it's like
To be told from birth your feelings are useless
and ball them up every single night
To be four years old and scared of the dark
simply, searching for some light
Told to be quiet and grow up – shut up your crying
You'll be aight

To throw a party on your 7th birthday and invite 15 of your Anglo friends

To sit at the edge of that table and recognize those Anglos ain't your friends
To be a nigger and a midget at least three times each in the same class transition
To have the entire world tell you you're nothing unless you're winning
To have winning narrowly defined within the scope of bars or a ball
Did I mention I lack humanity?
Or I ain't shit cause I ain't tall?

To be told to validate everyone's feelings but your own
To be reminded every second that you truly walk alone
To be ostracized because you know every word to that song that says I walk alone
To be too Black to know the names of every member of Green Day
To be too White to know that the name of Ike's challenger was Adlai

I guess you gotta get filled with lead by the cops for folks to really say your name
An elongated backspace in life
but a hashtag once you pass away

#AndMaybeThatsAllThatMatters

Manchild

Pain, Bineo Rideaux[4]

At twelve years old,

I was told

"You're the man of the house now."

---

[4] Bino Rideaux. "Pain." *No Pressure*, All Money In No Money Out, 2017.

How fuckin stupid is that?

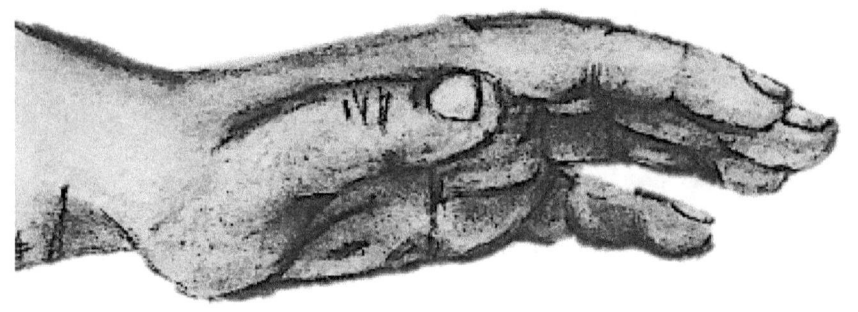

My Lawfully Wedded

A Couple of Forevers, Chrisette Michelle [5]

I am looking for a helper, not a squeeze, main, chick or whore, but a helper.

And lets be clear about a few things, because I know that you're wondering: she will not be perfect. She will have insecurities and sometimes be irritable for no apparent reason. She will not look like a model on the cover of *Vogue* or *Vanity Fair*. Her lips will be big and bold, and probably not as lush or firm as the women from those cable television primetime shows. She will prefer to wear flats because heels make her feet hurt. Her breast will sag, if she even has noticeable breast, and she will have dozens of stretch marks before she's even two months pregnant with our first child. She will talk, probably more than I would like, causing me to be emotionally disconnected from some of the biggest games of the years. She will at times find herself upset at me for reasons I do not fully know or understand. She will have acne. She will be subconscious about her body. She will overcook at least one meal once a week. She will not play videogames. She will pretend to like football but will relish the first Monday of every February. She will snore louder than me. She will look incredibly different on the morning of our tenth wedding anniversary than she does on our second date….

Need I say more?

I recognize these things. I concede many of them as truths. And even though there are many other factors that will come to realization, some mentioned above and some not yet thought of, here's what I am certain of: Mrs. Curtis will not be a perfect human being. She will be fallible. She will be sinful. She will sometimes be prideful and even more often

---

[5] Michele, Chrisette, OAK, Kenneth Gamble, Leon Huff & Andrew "Pop" Wansel. "A Couple of Forevers." *Better*, Universal Motown, 2013.

be selfish, and she will relentlessly scheme ways to get whatever she feels she wants.

Now that we got that out of the way, lets explore the possibilities.

Because for every so called "negative" that the bone of my bone shall have impressed upon her, the virtues she encompasses will shine ever so brighter.

She will be God-fearing. She will put her love, worship and adoration for the Lord above me. She will know how to pray for our children and me. She will lift my parents up. When I get short tempered and curse at her for no apparent reason, she will seek the Lord on my behalf, asking for his intercession and for forgiveness. She will inspire me to be a better man. She will make work and life easier. She will make yokes and burdens lighter to bear. With her I will experience ecstasy. I will love her even harder in the areas she is most insecure. I will show her the same grace God has shown me when she becomes irritable. She won't look like Sanna Lathan or Scarlett Johannson after multiple filters and Photoshop, but she will be the most beautiful girl in the world. I will long to make her feel like she's the only woman on Earth. She'll think her laugh is the most annoying thing in the world, but I'll hear it in my sleep. She will remind me of my purpose when I am laden with defeat. She will point me to the Cross when my behavior gets sporadic. She will be a wonderful mother. Her smile will radiate every room she walks into. She will be just as attractive, just as sexual and desirable, at forty-six as she is she is as twenty-eight. She will know when and how to put me in my place: sometimes sternly, other times minced with patience and grace, but all the time lovingly, in her own peculiar way.

I will not merely wait for you, because you desire to be pursued, but I will pursue the will of my Father first, romanticizing and courting you thereafter. And that pursuit will not end, because I will continue to date you; continue to impress you; continue to give you cheap gifts that I spent weeks putting together in my mind; continue to put your desires and necessities above that of my own; continue to love those things which are dearest to your heart and a part of your utmost affections.

She is by no means perfect, but she'll be perfect for me; and I'll be perfect for her; and we'll be perfect for each other. And we'll understand that perhaps marriage isn't meant to make us happy, but rather its designed to make us holy, and in our collective pursuit of holiness and sanctification, we will experience an abundant joy as a result of our union. We will wrestle, physically and theologically. We'll know one another's biggest dreams and greatest fears. She will make her dreams mine, and my dreams shall become hers. We'll adorn gloomy Saturday's together. We'll cook meals with one another. We'll set countdown clocks on our phones, anticipating the seconds left until one of us comes home from off the road. We'll take vacations, sometimes overseas, other times to the beach, perhaps downstairs to the basement, but regardless of the location, paradise will ensue, because we'll be wrapped in each other's arms. In those moments, there won't be a single care in the world, and if there is, she'll make it easier to handle. We'll help one another see our sin. We'll pray for true, genuine repentance. She will be emotional, and rather than complaining about that, I will embrace it. We'll have our ups and downs and our failures. We will not be perfect. There will be times when she cannot stand me, and I her. Over the course of a lifetime, there will be temptations, for me other women, for her other men. But we will stand firm to the promises of our lives, first to God, secondarily to one another; always reminded of the covenant we created in the eyes of our creator.

And none of this will be easy. Tears will be shed along the way. Jobs may be lost. Loans may be defaulted on. Friends and family will pass away from this life. We will be passed up for promotions and businesses may fail. Elections might be lost. Churches may decide to move in different directions. Children may get sick. We may fall ill.

But she will be my rock; my love; my queen, and I will remind her of this often. And I will be her king; her protector; her provider; treating her like Christ has treated me. Together, we will display an earthly depiction of eternity, and our friends, family, children, colleagues and associates will come to know the love of Christ because of our love for one another.

This is my prayer. This is what I shall wait for. My lover, my helper and my bestfriend.

Until that moment in time…

The Body

Hopeless Romantic, Wiz Khalifa feat. Swae Lee
[6]

I believed all the lies
About fellowship and vulnerability
About trust, compassion, courage
About love, family
About this oh so great gift of singleness
Even tho there ain't no ceremonies for singles
I believed it
Stupidity

My legs no where to be found
They left
Turned left down a Baltimore one way
They said follow me right before the light turned green
I tailed closely
Then the green faded into yellow
They turned
And I got stuck at the red
and left on read
to never see them again
Trustworthiness now confined
to the expediency of a wheelchair

---

[6] Wiz Khalifa, Swae Lee, Spruiell, Marcus, CBMIX, Young Chop. "Hopeless Romantic." *Rolling Papers 2,* Taylor Gang/Atlantic, 2018.

I try to roll it
I just can't
My hands numb from the arthritis of blind trust
The blood clots there
My heart don't flow
It's cold
I believed.

Arms invisible
Searched for any sight of em
I looked under the bed on Saturday morning
Anita Baker and Sadé playing
Sending text of desperation
Bout my need for company and affection
It goes ignored
Kinda like a Black boy telling his mother he's depressed
Just pray it away

No torso in tact
once mended by the deepest
of tragedies, the most neccesary of functions
But she found someone else to more intimately function
And once I was no longer the go to
for banking and boyfriend assistance
I became relegated to once upon a time mistress
Losing intimacy
All the while wondering what happened to my empathy
Just be content in Christ

And so, I believed

All that remains is my brain
And my mind is like a flesh eating pirhana
The body the barrier forcibly holding me back
Cept it's gone now
So it seeks out prey
Lashing out
Reminding me of my worthlessness
measure of imperfection
I don't see them as gifts
I lose power to hold off the beast
It swims freely
Like Ross Barnett's son at a pool
in Philadelphia, Mississippi
Circa 1953
And I want to name my daughter Zora
Yet eternally fearful that no matter how brilliant she may be
still buried in an unmarked grave
Disconnected from the body
all because I don't have that special somebody
But I got razor blades
And I'm not leaving Earth today
But I'm a alter this here body
I prayed bout it at the altar,
and on second thought,
maybe I'll alter this here body after all
once,
and for all.

This I Know

Moments, Jhene Aiko feat. Big Sean
7

I haven't written this for anyone in particular

I yet to know your name
or hairstyle
or the day you graced this place

Haven't explored your favorite color
Your laugh isn't ethced into my brain
Your scent doesn't linger in my imagination even when you're 2600 miles away

I don't know the depth of your pain and trauma
or who hurt you
in the past
Whether me calling your moms ma'am will drive her up the wall until she finally gets it
If your pops loves the World Cup or the Super Bowl
cause you can't equally love both
Or if you even have your parents around

I can't yet distinguish your voice in a room full of dancers
No beauty marks to envision gazing at when things get hard

---

[7] Aiko, Jhené, Anderson, Sean, Johnson, Amaire. "Moments." *Trip*, Def Jam Recordings, 2017.

No perfect memorization of the
curvature of your waistline when I wrap my arms around it
No discernment yet
bout your navel
your midriff
or your inner thigh
And what places are the ultimate spots
to rest my head when the world has beaten me down and my
respite is found in everything that is you

Don't know your favorite fragrance
How many socks, shirts and hoodies I'll never get back
I don't know the simulatenous warmth and butterflies
that exude from my insides when our lips so
Perfectly and Passionately align

I can't waist for the first time. My imaginations runnin' wild.

I mean, I can scheme, but I don't know our kids' names
How many we'll even have
Whether we'll be able to have any
what the depth of such a heartbreak would feel like

I don't know if you're even ready for me; if we're ready for each other; if I'm ready for you

But this I know…

I am waiting for you.
I am praying for you.

And I will love you,
as long as we both shall live.

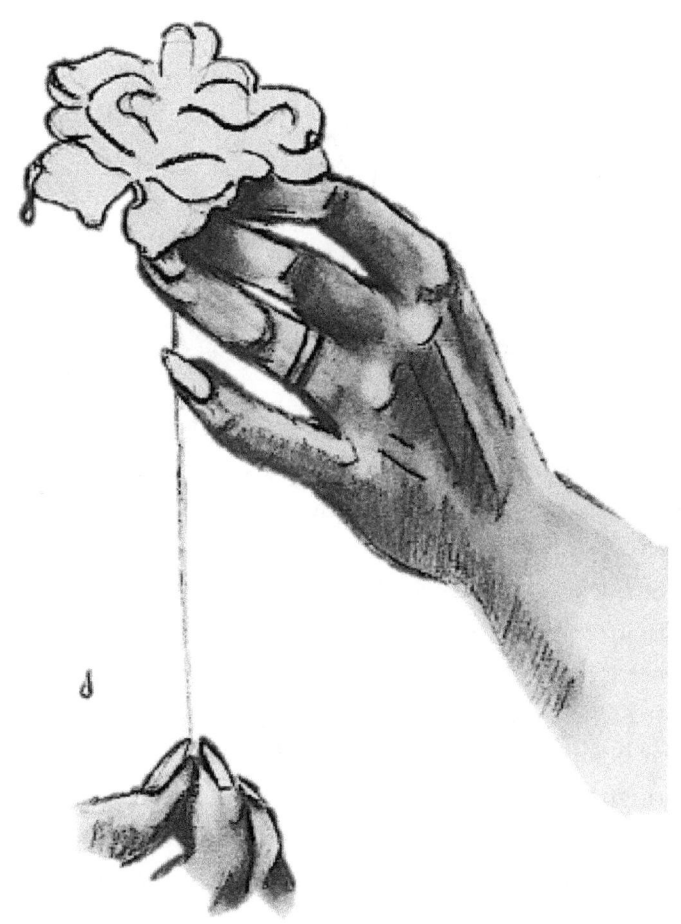

A Rose Is Still A Rose

Hate Being Sober, Chief Keef feat. 50 Cent & Wiz Khalifa
[8]

"But what if I can't find a job, bro?"
The deep layers of my skin blurt in unison.

There's this photo of Marilyn Monroe
And I like all the things about the 60's
I'm fascinated, minus the Black folks being
lynched and segregated against –
oh, and redlining … minus the redlining part too

    She's looking down at this flower
    a rose to be exact
    Her background abstract,
    obscured by greenery
    Greener pastures await.
    A great actress in wait,
    that being the deepest desire of her heart
    though she never secured the part she wanted most
    And she's looking down, in a sky blue halter top
    eerily reminiscent of the paleness in the sky above
    clouded by foilage
    yet not a cloud in the sky

---

[8] Jackson, Curtis, Cozart, K, T. Pittman, Thomaz, C.J.. "Hate Being Sober." *Finally Rich (Deluxe)*, Interscope Records, 2012.

      Ms. Mariyln secures self-actualization
      Least,
      that's the way I see it
          And all because this pink little rose
              Collarbone and chest out
              No matter how strenuous, exhausting, hopeless times may be
              Take heed
              ALWAYS FIND YOUR ROSE

"But what if you can't find a job?"
The "mentor" I've spoken to once in my life echoes
out of sheer rigidity

Tree…

"But what if you can't find your dream job?"
She asks. I leave the message on read
Boarding my flight to Heathrow

Landscape…

"But what if you can't secure the job?"
My mother asks cautiously

              An ode to insecurities.
              A gospel of sorts.
              Though not *the* gospel.
              A compass without arrows.
              A clock without hands.

A rose without thorns.
A track with no train.
A mountain with no trees.

    Sugar, let me tell you somethin'
    We done hit rock bottom before,
    in **every** phase of life
    at the Same Damn Time
    and when that happens,
    perspective is no longer elusive

I sat in the car one day,
neglected to find my rose.
Instead, I purchased a pack of razor blades
Thought about the things I would never do
Dreams never accomplished
Hopes dashed
Fears made true
Completely resigned to the finality of the moment

ALWAYS, FIND YOUR ROSE

What If I Love My Wife Too Much?

Fantasy, Mariah Carey
9

Excuse me for being in my feelings a lot lately. I'm not normally this kind of guy. I watch a lot of sports and enjoy a good beer, so that's enough for me to meet my daily requirement for societal masculinity, right?

Anyway, I wrote a little piece on relationships the other day. You know, how finding "the one" (whatever that means) is just as much about His perfect timing as ours. And as I realized that one of the more important things about finding a mate is actually something I have no control over, I got to thinking about something else. What if I love my wife *too* much?

I know, I shouldn't be thinking about it, and honestly, I'm not. Law school is annihilating my joyful existence at the moment, and I have a ton of work to get done before my family gets here for Thanksgiving. But, at the same time, I am thinking about it, and it's kind of frustrating.

I have a friend. She's a really good friend. (At least, I think she is.) We don't talk on a daily basis, or maybe not even as frequently as I would like. Heck, she may not even consider me a friend, but that's not important. I realized a few months back that as much as I love talking with her, that communication just can't take place as frequently as I would like. I like this friend, and she knows I like her, and this is

---

[9] Carey, Mariah, Belew, Adrian, Frantz, Christopher, Hall, Dave, Stanley, Steven, Weymouth, Tina. "Fantasy." *Daydream,* Columbia Records, 1995.

where that romantic attachment ends. Maybe she likes me too, but that's not important either. This friend really wants love, but I'm not sure it's a kind of love you can find outside a romantic relationship. That's the premise that is difficult for me to reconcile.

I want a friend. Odds are, you want one too. A friend you can escape to in time of emotional need. A friend that understands your quirkiness and engages you in useless conversation. A friend that listens to all of your stories, even though you've told them this same story four times before. (And yet, they *never* tell you that you have already shared it, they just listen intently the fourth time like they did on the first.) You know, someone to be vulnerable with, and feel completely safe and honest with. A friend that makes me feel like it's okay to believe I can literally fly, even though I know that by jumping off that two story building, I will probably break both legs and rupture my spleen. You know, it's that incapacitating, all-encompassing, emotionally riveting friendship that, somewhere along the way, we're all subconsciously told we want. (And, therefore, we consciously tell ourselves that we *need*.)

I don't think romance *has* to be a part of that friendship, but then sometimes, I think it does. I have some really great friends. They are actually the best friends in the world. They listen to me. They intercede on my behalf. They offer me food and ask me about my little brother. They love me, and I feel that love down to the marrow in my bones. But even after years of unconditional love and a series of moments when they have proven their loyalty to me, I still have this tiny bit of reservation. It's as if I want us to go deeper, but I'm scared. My fear doesn't stem from being afraid of getting hurt, but from some other, non-descriptive element that I can't quite qualify. (So perhaps that's what this is about, me openly sorting through this lack of understanding.)

That friend I described, the friend I *really* want, I know they exist, but I'm compelled to believe that that friend has to be a woman, and that I can't really experience that level of intimacy in a friendship unless there's also a similar level of intimacy between the two of us. How did I come to this conclusion? The friend I have, the one that I can't talk to as much as I would like, has a romantic partner. Somewhere along the way, we decided (without consulting with one another) that our friendship had to have limitations. These limitations aren't out of a sexual desire, but more so out of protecting emotions. Guarding your heart is about way more than closing your legs and keeping your loins in your pants.

I love her, but I have this raging desire within me to *love* her, and when someone else gets a chance to love her in the way I want to, the only way our relationship could remotely feel complete is if I too had someone else to share the intricacies of life with. It sucks. Maybe we should just be together. Maybe I should just call her this evening and be vulnerable and pour my heart out and let her know just how much I want to be *the* friend in her life, but I can't do that. I won't do that. I got too much pride. She's got too many months invested in the current guy. So, as a result, we both keep looking for this friend, even though I'm not sure either of us knows that friend exist.

You see, I want all of my friendships to be deeper. I want to trust people more. I want to feel like it's okay for me to have an increased level of vulnerability, but there's that little nudge that offers a huge brush of resistance. I know that, unless this friend turns out to be *the* friend, there will always be limitations to our vulnerabilities. That's not always a bad thing. You don't tell all of your friends everything. Some friends are good at listening about family issues, while others can relate to the joys of the legal field; some are particularly good at talking sports. In essence, you don't need one person to be *everything* to you. That would be a mundane life, and one settled on a fast track to disaster.

But when it comes to sharing dreams and fears, and articulating my sincerest hopes and visions of the world that I hope to leave, I just don't feel like I can share that with anyone yet, because I'm afraid that one day, I'll eventually have to share her.

You know how people say sit back, relax and marry your best friend? Well, that's the goal. That doesn't mean someone has to be your best friend for years before you are romantic, but it does mean that that person ought become the closest confidant in your life. A person who makes the burdens in life seem like the oceans waves at the shore, mere ponds for navigation until the next one comes through. A person that knows what you're thinking before you say it, that understands how to make you feel appreciated and valued and important in the world – and senses when you need to feel these things the most. These things, they don't have to come from a romantic partner, but then again, they kind of do. At least, I feel like they do, because if I somehow find this in a platonic partnership, it means that, in all likelihood, I risk the chance of losing these securities to someone else. That's a risk I'm just not sure I'm willing to take.

I've fantasized about this woman for some time now. I've got this vague idea about who she is, what she desires and what life with her will bring about. And I've explored these thoughts and feelings so much that it's starting to make me sick to my stomach, as if fairytales can only keep their subtle dispositions subtle for so long, if for no other reason than the four year old eventually turns twenty-four.

Society, the church, and my friends and family have, without intention, helped me fall deeply in love with someone that doesn't even exist yet. For a minute I thought this couldn't be real, and then I surveyed my heart, and evaluated all of the reservations I already have in place, all for this woman who may or may not exist. Am I delusional?

One of the biggest goals I have in life is to be able to tell myself at the end that I loved one woman with a fervent and unconditional love that I never gave to anyone else. I pointed her to God. I was faithful to her. I protected and cherished her. I held her hand at sporting events and painted her toenails on snowy Winter nights. I woke up at 4 am and drove thirty-seven miles to the closest IHOP when she was seven months pregnant, just so she could cure a particular pancake craving. I loved her – as she is, as she later became, and as she was, all of the time, and I wish to do this with no questions asked, or reservations in hand. But a part of me kind of feels like this is too much, like it's slightly creepy to love someone *that* hard, you know, before they even argue with you for no reason at all.

Anyway, this is me: thinking aloud, sifting through my emotions, longing for intimacy and vulnerability, with someone who I don't even know, and a person that doesn't know me.

I think I'll go have a Yuengling and watch NFL Network – more than enough emotions for a few days.

Windy

Keep Ya Head Up, 2Pac[10]

Sometimes I just stand
on the sidewalk
and sometimes, in the middle of racing
to the next destination
Souls lagging,
many wishin they didn't even exist

I wonder if she cuts herself
If he beats her then holds her hand
Is the lady driving the minivan ready to gulp Xanax?

What direction?

If only I could rewind
Erase infinte transgressions
Balance out the seesaw of
chemicals in my brain
Alter the medula
Teardrops live there

---

[10] 2Pac, Anderson, D., Troutman. "Keep Ya Head Up." *Strictly 4 My N.I.G.G.A.Z....*, Interscope Records, 1993.

Navigation – no.
Pavement – no.
Pot holes a bliss.
Repent.

We'll claw
Cry
pant endlessly
nothing changes
Wind.
Winds a blowin'

A Moment in Paradise (it's fleeting until it's right)

Whipped Cream, Ari Lennox
[11]

Dearest,

I spent last week taking a break from everything. I did not write. I did not study. I did not explore potential business endeavors or conjure up additional political strategies. Instead, I rested. I spent time with you, with our friends. It was wonderful. It was magical. It was just what I needed.

The day we both knew we were going to dread has finally arrived. We knew it would come, but it seemed so deep into the distance that I'm not sure either of us ever properly prepared for it. Then again, I don't think you really prepare for things like this. The best thing to do is to live in the moment, live *for* the moment, and be frivolous with your love, sacrificial with your heart, and vulnerable with your emotions. I have done that. You have done that. *We* have done that.

In some ways, our trip symbolized the end of one chapter of life and the beginning of another. At first glance, that moves us to a level of unexplainable despondency, but it doesn't have to. It shouldn't. There's finality to all things in life, even life itself, and I think the only way to truly be at peace, to live freely, lovingly and comfortably, is to embrace that finality. This chapter of our life is over, and a new one is set to begin, but it's just that, *our* life.

---

[11] Salter, Courtney, Parrino, Anthony, Blackmon, Larry, Gilmore, Ronald, Croker, Theo. "Whipped Cream." *Shea Butter Baby*, Dreamville/Interscope Records, 2019.

I did this with someone else three years ago, and knew then the complete opposite of what I know now. That couldn't work. This can. This will. But even if some unforeseen circumstance decides to exert itself in our life, nothing or no one can ever change or takeaway what I feel right now; what I felt last week; what I have held onto lately.

In the past, I thought of paradise as a location, a place you travel to, with crisp white sand and beautifully clear water. I've been to a lot of places like that, and as nice as they may be, as serene as the sound of the waves as they wash up to the shore, the waves don't make me feel the way you do. The sound of the birds chirping in the morning cannot compete with the octaves of your voice. The beauty of the sunset can't compare to the beauty that is you.

You have shown me more than I can truly thank you for in our time together. I cannot articulate my gratitude. I cannot illustrate my love. That, however, will not stop me from trying to do so.

Who knows what the future holds. I would love for it to include you, to include *us*: building successful careers; raising beautiful children; doing life together. *Us*, struggling together; wondering at times if this will work; repenting of our sins; willing ourselves to love one another once more; being blissfully head over heels in the year 2045. *Us*: having petty arguments; fighting about who's going to clean the bathroom; me being ecstatic about you making partner, and you being happier than I am that we just won an election. *Us*: not being perfect, but being perfect for one another. I like *us*. I love *us*. This is what I want. This is what I need.

For now, the future and all of its wonders aside, know that you are loved. You are honored, adorned and cherished. You are a queen. You are my queen, and I love you so dearly.

The word paradise is still a noun. For me, it used to be a place. Now, it's a person. That person is *you*.

Positive Affirmations

You are not worthless
You are not a failure
You are worthy of life
You are worthy of love

How are you?

(Please use the space below to genuinely answer that question)

Maybe

Come and See Me, PARTYNEXTDOOR feat. Drake[12]

Maybe we were always afraid to make a baby but never shied away from the act of making one
Maybe that's where we got lost
Maybe in those moments,
while the television was on indiscriminately
or we turned the music loud enough so your parents or roommate wouldn't hear
Maybe that's where we got lost,
creating the perfect melody for our own breakup song
Maybe the entire thing was wrong
Maybe I was never the man I was supposed to be to you
Maybe I never pointed you to the heavens
Maybe the only thing I ever did right was keep my tongue right there,
perk my lips in soft spots
confirm that heaven has a g

Maybe I never deserved you
Maybe you were right
Maybe I never had a clue
Maybe I ran away from home and got degrees and worked three jobs because I never fully faced the trauma from the man in the mirror, and all of the people, wonders and reflections that shaped who and what I had become.

---

[12] Brathwaite, Jahron, Graham, Aubrey, Shebib, Noah. "Come and See Me." *PARTYNEXTDOOR3 (P3)*, OVO Sound/Warner Records Inc., 2016.

Maybe I never learned how to be vulnerable, and
I unfairly placed the burden of my fragile emotions on your shoulders,
as if you're so much older and don't have troubles in your life that I should
be helping you navigate along the way.

Maybe we should've rode the boat together
Maybe I should've been born a better man
I'm for sure I should've tried better to assist
and understand
Questioning my existence was never part of the plan
it just kind of came along

And for a brief moment in time you were a champion on the throne
And in hindsight, I'm certain that was the ultimate failing

Maybe things never felt right, and we both ignored our senses because everything about you was perfect, and even though I thought I was utterly worthless, I knew when your legs started shaking I meant something to someone, and the pet name hun was code for so many things, not least of which is making sure you come first. And maybe that's all wrong.

Maybe I made you an idol
Maybe I made this all up
Maybe one day I'll know
Maybe we can start over,
fall in love

#MeToo

Too Deep For the Intro, J. Cole
13

She told me it was
fine
That I'd be
fine
And she was
fine
So I said,
fine

At least,
in my mind, there's
no way I could decline.
Portioned a glass of wine
Said I deserve to unwind
..... then,
dem hips started to whine

After all, you the man of the house,
right?
Stressin' bout mortgages
gettin' paid
Weeds bein' clipped
Babies eatin' and bathin'

---

[13] J. Cole and Davis, Juro. "Too Deep for the Intro." *Friday Night Lights*, Dreamville & Roc Nation, 2010.

You a man,
what kinda man
ain't been with a lady?

You da father, brother
and husband
Only a son at practice
When that backtalk be too forward
I could see it.
I seent she visualized it,
weight on my shoulders
craters of the moon
Holes.
black like a galaxy
black like medieval plagues
black like that feeling of
being called a virgin at the cafeteria table

And her figure,
her figure was Black too
Hair Black, like Yara
Lips Black, like Niecy
Hips Black, like Serena
ass, too
Toes black w/white, gel polish
so we know what that mean

That weight so heavy
Heavy like that Toshiba black
TV stand
Scuffin my black forces up 110 floors
black smoke engulfing my lungs
Natural weight of being a Black boy

Feelin her weight to
simply let some weight off
Whispers,
"take my bra off"
And the minute her tongue
Connects on the creases of my neck
Erect
First time it's ever happened
Not on my own
Basement of my
Mother's home
Sixteen years old
With a 34 year old
Didn't know you had to slide the hook

Silhouettes Etched Across the Window Pane / The Orgasm Gap

Savage (Remix), Megan Thee Stallion feat. Beyoncé[14]
Come Thru, Summer Walker (with Usher)[15]

Apparently, they told her she needed to act, walk and talk a certain way, otherwise, God wouldn't love her, but even worse, no man would either.

And I can see how that would worry you, how it can make the marrow in your femurs quiver with uncontrollable terror.

But she got older, and fear turned into disgust, and she realized the sensation from the nerve endings in her toes to torso to every where in between, and, soon after, yes, she too could catch a nut.

And from that point on, she left the church behind. Said she ain't need "organized" religion. Said all she needed was her and god.

Matter fact, told me the other day that "my best friend fucked her man a week after they met. He put a ring on it six months later, and they been happily married

---

[14] White, Anthony, Beyoncé, Sessions Jr., Bobby, Hazzard, Brittany, Milano, Derrick, Thorpe, Jorden, Pete, Megan Thee Stallion, Carter, Sean, Nash, Terius, "Savage Remix." *Savage Remix*, 1501 Certified Ent. LLC, 2020.

[15] Charles, Nija, Robinson, Aubrey, Dupri, Jermaine, Bailey, Kendall Roark, Holmes, London, Seal Jr., Manuel, Walker, Summer, Raymond IV, Usher. "Come Thru." *Over It*, LVRN/Interscope Records, 2019.

for five years now. Y'all need to stop."

And yet her beloved friend, Mary, still never known a man, cept the few times she got lockjaw and such, a smidgen over 30, still single. Still alone.

And she said that's when it hit her, affirmed in a nutty way of sorts. I am a woman, and my value to man, woman or Being ain't determined by how many times I lay.

And I just kissed her on the cheek. With a one armed hug. And whispered "OK."

Woman

If I Was Your Woman, Alicia Keys
16

To infinity and beyond / that's how strong my love is / that's how perfect the boot fits

My eyes do a little rolling when you ride it [like a' cowgirl] / That's why I kiss you like I'll never see you again / adore your presence like Andy

Love and repair you through the brokenness and imperfections / Come up off that road dying – waitin' to see your [lip(s) &] smile / Guns blazin'

Wistfully wandering, wooing like the Wild West / like the sea, you engulf me / your legs the cage – I don't ever want to leave

I know how it feels to fly

---

[16] Bachararch, Burt, McMurray, Clarence, Jones, Gloria, David, Hal, Sawyer, Pam. "If I Was Your Woman/Walk On By." *The Diary of Alicia Keys*, RCA/JIVA Label Group, 2003.

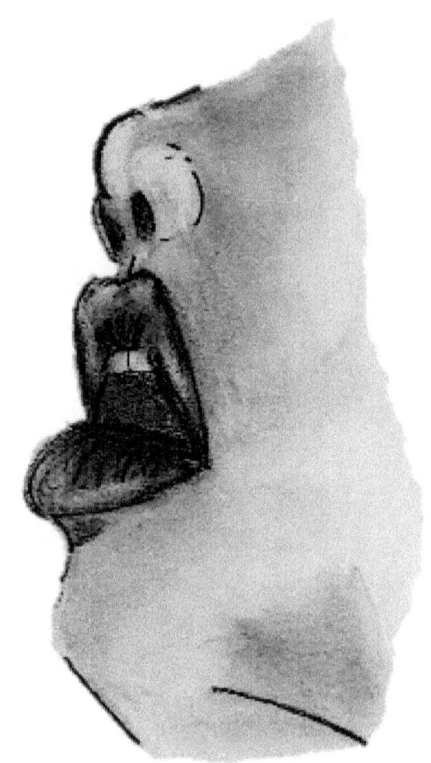

Mississippi Love Letter

Go To Town, Doja Cat[17]

Moans
masterful and magical
mystifying and mythical
a ritual
just between us two
I close my eyes
Grip Tight

Intellectual
incredibly and, yes,
indelible
    definitely edible
manicured claws wrap my head
all three sides of the taper
Grip Loosens periodically
long enough to inhale
like a vapor
then back to the job at hand
After all,
one who doesn't work,
don't eat

---

[17] Chahayed, Rogét, Dlamini, Amala Zandile, Sprecher, David, Powel II, Gerald A., Lewis, Rian. "Go To Town." *Amala*, Kemosabe Records/RCA Records, 2018.

Sensationally scintillating
Lima Tell You Bout this Color
glowing off her dark chocolate skin
seen it as she slid out the seat of the sedan
never written a love letter to a woman
that needed a tan
knew at that very moment what I wanted from the night
Metabolism fast
heart race increasing —
along with my appetite

Soothing and symptomatic
successfully quivering
arches flow.
legs sway.
Like bridges artificially do
Naturally, messes are to be cleaned
with a few fell swoops of the lapper
few times round the track suffices
Eventually, aggressively
shoving away her current vices
I insist on continuation
She can't do a pull-up, yet in these
moments, her upper body strength
rivals AI's durability
I'll never put my hands on her
but something's getting beaten up tonight

Infatuation incubates

Nestles into our space
REM fully settled in

                                          P for the shape I so endlessly make
                                          P for the pseudonym of what was endlessly ate

Instantaneously, invited into her arms
a kiss to seal the fate
until next time, my dear
as if we're both half a human being
unable to feel below
floating off into the abyss
we missed the midnight train hours ago

This How I Feel When Sza's Prom Come On

Prom, SZA[18]

Invisible to invincible
time not wasted
Contemplating forward thoughts?
That's a normal thing,
fixating our finite imagination

Like there's still time to love you.
To love on you.
Like there's still yet time to fall,
In love with you
All over again –
And again
    And again
        And again
           Like the brigde
on *That's What It's Made For*

Affirmation that there's good in goodbyes
cept the depth of the initial blow
long as we each get one more blow
and my resilience,

---

[18] Lang, Carter, Rowe, Solana, Donaldson, Tyran. "Prom." *Ctrl*, Top Dawg Entertainment, 2017.

shit, this goin' pass too
like all the other bullshit do.
We can.
We'll rise again.

Melodic hug wrapped round my heart
Wrap around porch squeezing so tight
tears collect. Ready to stream
down my eyes,
nestled tight in dem arms
I feel seen, loved, heard, redeemed
in these here arms of yours
Solid solace and respite
been absent since I left the nest,
chasing that dream they call college
all so I could hold a family down
I'm the bank, therapist, counselor,
oh, and a pastor, too
to all of 'em
so with the weight of the wait
and the world on my shoulders
I'll never be able to truly show ya
how much it means to me
That we put our weight on each other
and we wait on one another
serving and swirving in the car and the bed
between each other's eyes and our legs
you too feel so utterly and butterflying
Beautiful
the world you've created just for the two of us

I hope I never have to pull out

The validity of the nuance of
my sexuality. You holding my hand.
"You?"
    Pssh. You not no freak."
Why me?
One ubiqutious stare
riles inanimate senations.
Control thy self,
but what happens when neither of us want to?
I take one look and want to f*** you,

                                        and make love with you
                                        all in the same night
                                        All Night Long
                                        cause true love brings salvation
                                        I never knew that before you

Consequences fade into
distant memories,
especially in the moment, knowing
slip-ups alter plans. And we care.
but the way we hold one another,
it makes double lines worth it.
Squatting in parallel universes
for perpindicular purpose.
Say that now.
Say it deep down.
And mean it.
Pretending to dread it.

Passionately accept it.
And wanting me to feel as close as humanly possible

"That can't be sin, right?
Is that a crime?"

I decline to ponder further.
Hit decline on my phone.
Turns off lights and cuts the music on.
Is It a Crime is playing
helps level out the moans

Being enough for you is all I wanted in life
and I suppose we may not make it further,
what we had was way more than they could see
Sunsets always fade,
no matter how often they come
Winter's linger
maybe even, love dissipates
But at least I got to love ya
Forever young in each other's heart
And that matters
Cause the snow where we live
falls well into the spring
And older summer's in Miami
eventually overtake our dreams
But for now, since the snow still falling,
since we got nowhere to be,
since I'm the only friend for you
and you the only one for me

might as well drop to our knees?

You've done enough, lil' darlin
this one here?
It's on me

What Dat Mouf Do

No Limit, G-Eazy feat. Cardi B[19]*
*(but like, Cardi's verse *only*)

Quote scriptures
For God so loved the world
He gave his only begotten Son
She told me she believes that
Right before she said
This here, somebody's son,
bout to circle the globe between my legs
You know, that way there's no chance
for sperm to meet egg

Speak life
Tell my friends I love them when
they least expect it but need it most
Taste and see that the Lord is good
After all, something don't come from nothing
Besides, have you ever had chips and queso?
Dip the perfectly salted and still warm chip
into the divinely melted and seasoned cup
of melted dairy and pastuerized product

---

[19] Ritter, Allen, Almánzar, Belcalis, Taylor, Earl Patrick, Gillum, Gerald, Fort, Jay Anthony, Thorpe, Jordan, Fort, Klenord, Samuels, Matthew, Mayers, Rakim. "No Limit." *The Beautiful Diamond*, RCA Records, 2017.

Taste that, and tell me there ain't no God

Say oh my, oh my
When I see Teyana
hear her tell *me* to hurry
And I think to myself, what a wonderful world
And some folks say there's no God

Pray
even though it's really the Spirit
interceding on my behalf
with moanings and groanings man just
simply can't understand
But religion's created by man
so no more talking about the Son of Man
or how hard it is to be a man
or the pain of never knowing the fullness
of the man your bother could've/would've been
Take my hand, she says
Put it *here*
Her other pair of lips do the talking
pelvis thrusts interposing
These moans require no exegesis

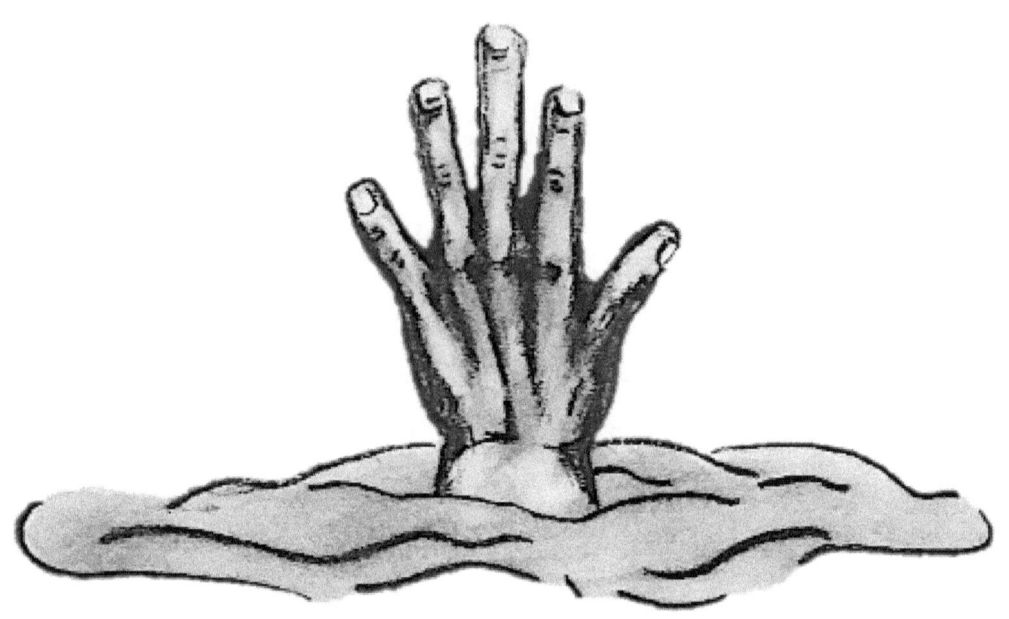

Bywater Blues

D'evils, Jay-Z[20]

All the residual pain makes my heart stop
Blood dripping like tears when they call the cops
Legs shaking no erasing what you been through
Ambition took you to the streets from the classroom
Ain't no telling when or how the story end though
I just wish I could've stayed met your kinfolk
I just wish I really I had a heart for the work
Everybody look at you like you don't know your worth
But you just say fuck 'em dawg, make they heart stop
I ain't speaking bout the shells when the case drop
I'm talkin Black excellence, build your business man
Went from $7.25 to a couple grand
Went from reading folk tales to measuring grams
Went from dappin Mr. Curtis to dappin up hands
On the corner cause the Franklins comin faster though
And Tatianna missed her cycle thought she'd let you know
And you been fuckin round even though you love her much
Thought bout fadin on her but you know how tough it is
To walk this world never knowing the love of your dad
Your mother hating it so much but you know she just sad
Cause that nigga told her he loved her and she felt that shit
Told him she was pregant and he said "I don't want that bitch"

---
[20] Jay-Z. "D'evils." *Reasonable Doubt*, S. Carter Enterprises, LLC, 1996.

I miss you, and all the lessons that we could've learned
Sometimes I can't sleep at night, espeically since I heard
Quiana caught a bullet, drive-by,
on the corner of Claiborne and Jourdan
Paramedics took an hour not givin a damn
Held her hand while the pavement went from scorched to ice cold
Reminiscing on the times I had to give you a scold
And how you're becoming the most beautiful young lady the Lord could ever mold
Success told, prep made, thank God you survived
Looking in your eyes, wishing we could switch sides
Paralyzed and hopeless, and can't do nothing but stand on the other side
Resentment boiling like water, wishing I had died

But somehow you rose up from the gutter
My students the main reason I love roses like Paula love butter
Cause my lil niggas been niggers but it ain't slow them down
It ain't keep em from believing they can change they town
It ain't keep my ladies from knowing and loving more of they self
Knowing what's between they legs don't determine they wealth
And still, I feel like I let you down, love
I pray to God we recognize each other when we make it up above

The South Will Rise Again

Ronald Reagan Era, Kendrick Lamar[21]

…. But me?
I walk across the street with the confidence of a middle aged
White man.
Heterosexual, of course.
Blue eyes.
Blond hair so fluffy you would think it's
cotton as I part my hand through
Chief executive of the downtown high rise
Chief executors of thievery and insecurity
Explicitly cruel via the door of no return
My ancestors discerned,
treated lower than cattle
Chains, whips, scars
cuts and brusies
And I ain't talking white meat, few stitches
burnin' in the shower for a week
Nah….
I'm talking infectious, puss trickling out at the
mere pressing against a white shirt
End of day sweating and the wounds,

---

[21] Duckworth, Kendrick Lamar. "Ronald Reagan Era." *Section.80*, Top Dawg Entertainment/Section.80, 2011.

the wounds reopen cause the scabs peel away and stay woven
In the cotton
can't sleep
the flies are feeding off thine flesh

Sometimes I use the crosswalk
Other moments I don't
Depends on how I feel
Ray bans my Tuesday frames
Chipotle for lunch
Don't think twice bout the guac
Knows the previous ten year yield of the S&P 500
but too damn lazy to pronounce Akeliah correctly
You see,
I don't look both ways before crossing the street
Why should I?
Great great great granddaddy owned slaves on 40 acres
Great great grandad used the Irish for cheap labor
Grandad went to school on the GI bill
Bought a house off the Homestead Act
Had retirement from Social Security
Had no competition in the workforce
Lived out by the lake,
near the highest elevation in the city
Signed a covenant with the neighbors
"No Negroes here" (in sign)
"No Niggers here" (in conversation)
Probably threw a brick through Haddie Mae and Leonard's house
when they tried to move in
But hard work.

All they did was work so hard.

So I walk across the street like I'm invincible
Like death will never know my name
Like I've earned everything in life
Like I'm God's singular and precious gift to creation

Jesus looks like me, ya know.
After all, aren't we all made in the
image of a blond haired, blue eyed God?

<u>Black Men Don't Have the Luxury of Fearing Death</u>

King Kunta, Kendrick Lamar[22]

So, I've got quite the story to tell....

I've long been debating whether or not to get a tattoo on my hand. There's a very specific design I want, and I have put it off longer than I truly wanted. In fact, back in 2013 at one of those "sit down and watch me talk about how great I am" law clerk lunches, an attorney pulled me to the side at the end and said "unless you plan on getting into entertainment, you should keep the tattoos to a minimum. It's just the rules." I proceeded to get my entire right arm and chest done over the next four years. I make my own rules.

Fast forward to tonight. I'm driving home from the gym, you know, the gym that I was leaving at 10:30 pm because I didn't leave my fancy office job until 8:30 pm. You know, the office job where I get to tell people about my fancy law degree, bathe in intellectual artifacts of self-importance, and brag about all the dignitaries across the country whose cell phone numbers I have in mine. Oooo child, that job so fancy.

As I'm headed home, Anne Arundel County's finest puts his lights on, right as I was merging on I-97. I stopped immediately, threw the hazards on. Sometimes

---

[22] Bruner, Stephen, Burns, Johnny, Duckworth, Kendrick, Gordy, Stefan, Jackson, Michael, Lewis, Ahmad. "King Kunta." *To Pimp a Butterfly*, Aftermath/Interscope Records, 2015.

you think you know why you're being stopped, but 50% of the time, at least for Black men, there is no reason, other than your skin tone.

AA's finest proceed to approach the vehicle. The first cop had called for backup before he got out the car, so they approach the front of the vehicle, each with their arms noticeably on their weapons, one on each side. I roll the window down, and AA one ask for license and registration. I oblige, but not before I tell him explicitly "Yes, officer, I have my wallet in my coat pocket, and my registration in the glovebox. I will now reach for my pocket, and then the glovebox." You know, because if I don't give explicit directions, any sudden movement is justification to blow my head off. Be respectful to the police, they said. Everything will be fine, they said. Except Philando ain't here to say a damn thing.

Anyway, AA one asks me if I have any idea why I'm being stopped. I literally have no idea. I mean, I have an idea (I'm Black, duh) but as far as a legit, lawful idea, nah, there is none. AA one tells me he pulled me over because "your left tailight is out." Which is odd. It's strange. Quite frankly, it's a lie, and I know it's a lie. At my real fancy, suit wearing job, I park in a garage, and I *always* back in, which means I can see the reflection of both tailights, every morning and every night.

AA one then proceeds to ask if I have any bombs, contraband or other explosives or devices he should be worried about. I wanted to be like "yeah, I keep a couple boxes of C4 in my trunk on the regular." But I say no sir, you know, just like Emmett did, probably before he realized there weren't enough sirs to keep the center block from weighing his body down to the bottom of the water.

So AA one goes back to the car to run the license and registration, while AA two remains standing on the passenger side, hand still on his firearm. After about seven minutes, AA two leaves, returns to his car, and speeds off. Guess I'm no longer a threat to anyone's life. No need for backup. Hopefully the shells from the nine don't tear my back up tonight.

AA one comes back. I roll my window down. "Sir, have you ever been arrested." I say no. You know, I'm a model citizen. I done everything Reagan and Jerry Falwell and the rest of them folks say is right for the Colored folk to come out of poverty, move up the social ladder and such. But wait, AA one isn't done, because then he says "Well there was a Frederick Curtis arrested back in '02 in Howard County, but no date of birth." Mind you, I was eleven years old in 2002. But in 1932, little 11 year old Black boys used to get hung from trees, simply because they didn't say sir or ma'am. And it was just last year, some hundred years later, where we built a place where the world could say their names.

So AA one lets me go, says it's a warning, even says he was going to write the citation but "the printer didn't print it correctly."

I get home. Taillight isn't out, like I knew the whole time.

But this story has a happy ending. I don't write about all my police stops. If I did, I'd have nothing else to write about. But now, whether or not I get ink on my hand is totally dependent on how I feel next time I'm in a shop. Because I've discovered this principle in life, that being, there's no fancy degree, job, salary or prestige that can make racist accept you. The world don't work that way. And I'm OK with that. If y'all hadn't noticed, it's why I do what I want to do, when I want to do it, how I want to do it. I'm not afraid of anyone or anything telling me they no longer want or need me. I'm a Black man. I have to make my own way in this world regardless, and I don't have the luxury of fearing death.

And that concludes my quite long winded story. I'm glad I got to tell her, and I got another entry in my poetry book. But I can't help but think about all the young men my age, my skin color, who will never be able to tell the story of their bogus, unlawful, racist traffic stop. I'll keep getting and pinning ink, just for you, my brother. Be love.

Episodic

1-800-273-8255, Logic feat. Alessia Cara, Khalid[23]

1

    I woke up this morning.
    Bright eyed. Attacking the day with an enthusiasm unknown to mankind. Reading my Bible and praying to my God. Drinking my coffee with agave nectar as the sweetner, and only one teaspoon of all-natural organic creamer. Got my run in. Put my lotion on. Moisturized between my legs, too. Like that beautiful Black woman I woke up to. Made love to her. Grabbed her neck and licked her toes. Put the tip of my tongue on every stretch mark I could find. Made my bed. Did the hard things first. Did the easy things with detail. Even met a friend for lunch. Met another friend for happy hour. Called another friend after dinner. Told her I loved her. Even wrote a poem and said a prayer for my brother.

2

    I woke up this morning.
    Answered the emails I've been neglecting. Thinking about the meaning of life. Frustratingly annoyed by the smallest things. Recalibrating myself. Empathy I'm not equipped to manage today. Half my to-do list done. Three cups of coffee by lunch. Internal discontent from her external annoyance that I just can't match her energy today. No matter how hard I try. Thought about writing a chapter. Played FIFA instead. Asked God what's the purpose of all this.

3

---

[23] Caracciolo, Alessia, Taggart, Andrew, Ivatury, Arjun, Wiggins, Dylan, Robinson, Khalid, Hall II, Robert Bryson Hall. "1-800-273-8255." *Everybody*, Def Jam Recordings, 2017.

I woke up this morning.

Pressed snooze fifty leven times. Stared over and over again at the post-its littered on my walls. Telling myself that I'm not worthless. That I'm not a failure. That I am worthy of life. That I am worthy of love. Over and over and over again. Listening to Jamila Woods. Reading Eve Ewing. Blasting Nip. Looking down at the scars on my wrist. Thinking they're not so fresh now.

4

I woke up this morning.

Aimlessly searching for my rose. Getting the feeling they've all died. Thinking they're never coming back. Wishing I could be normal. Crying. Inside and Out. Rationalizing my thoughts. Meticuously crafting how I might take my life. Checking to see if my brother's estate gets the life insurance payout if the blade slashes just right. Went for a night run. Wearing all black.

5

I woke up this morning.

Got out of bed. Stared out the same window for two hours and eleven minutes straight. Made a sandwich. Ate half of it and then couldn't eat anymore. Didn't go back to the kitchen the entire day. Called a friend. Lied about how I was doing. Told them business is good. Told them I'm doing fine. Stared somemore out the window. Saw my laundry piling up. Thought about the bills that need to be paid. All the people I've hurt. All the tears I've shed.

6

I woke up this morning.

Trembling with shivers in a warm and humid room. Stoic from yesterday's tears. Phone dead for nine hours. Pillow my only confidant. Television off and discreet. Silent. A black hole. Like my existence. I can only make it to the bathroom.

7

I woke up this morning.
I hope I don't tomorrow.

8

I woke up this morning.
And that's enough.
And that's OK.

One More Light

Triggers.

All I can think about nowadays are triggers.

I've been spending a lot of time with Cassandra, or San for short. She's my all-world therapist, and she's the only thing keeping me alive right now – aside from my four little girls. I stopped seeing San shortly after it happen. I figured it wouldn't help. Nothing would help, and talking about it was least helpful of all.

Except, I can't get my mind off of it. But that doesn't matter. I can't stop thinking about it, but it doesn't help to talk about it, so I just prefer to obsess over the very thing I know I will never forget.

Every thing is a goddamn trigger.

I took the girls over to their Aunt Rachel's house last night, and as we piled out of the car into the split level ranch, I saw that Rach had went out and secured their favorite – a party nugget tray from Chick-Fil-A. The oldest, Olivia, helped unfasten the little ones — two year old Ilyana and four year old Trenta. (I call her

Trent — should've never added the "A") Eight year old Elena, who I'm convinced is turning 39 this July and not 9, helped secure the bags from the trunk. As the girls gathered at the living room table, Olivia distributed paper plates as Rach nestled the tray onto the middle of the table.

"Eye" Rach said in my direction. No one I know calls me by my full name, Ayesha, preferring instead to use a one syllable spinoff that's prounced "I" but my mother decided would be better if spelled with three words. "Can you hand that bag of sauces?"

I lifted the thin bag, filled to the brim with every sauce imaginable. I picked up Ilyana and placed her in the high chair at the kitchen table, filling her plate with nuggets and stealing one or two along the way.

"Can I have some polynesian sauce?" Olivia asked.

And that's when it hit.

The sudden rush of emotion and grief and angst slowly warped and encompassed my entire being. I have never been a cryer. I pride myself on not being emotional. Even though I don't see anything wrong with it, I made a pact with myself that when my husband died, I would be strong for my girls, and in my twisted, never-ending grieving state, part of that strength meant not letting them see me shed tears. But ever since Curt's death, I haven't been able to hold true to that personal promise. I can't stop crying, in the same way I can't stop being numb and angry all at once.

Curt loved polynesian sauce. He loved Chik-Fil-A. We would joke all the time about how he'd stop being a whore one of these days and find a nice woman and settle down, and that his wedding would be catered by Chik-Fil-A. Curt took it another step forward one time, suggesting that instead of drink options like Jack Daniels and lemonade, the resturaunt's sauces would be the only liquid offerings. "Polynesian sauce will be a drink option, not merely for dipping." he joked. For some reason I believed him.

I passed Olivia the sauce, holding my tears long enough to run upstairs in a way that seemed only marginally hasty.

"What's wrong with mommy, Auntie?" I could hear Trent ask as I wallowed up the steps and into the master bathroom.

"I think she's sad" Oliva surmised.

"Mommy went upstairs to take a little break." Aunt Rachel offered as an explanation. "She'll be back down soon. Let's all eat before the fries get cold."

———

There's no naivety or dumbing down of the situation in the Davies family. Ayesha and Rachel and all the adults know the kids know, for the most part, aside from little Iylana of course. They've had the difficult conversations ad nauseam in the days since, and have cried more tears in the middle of the night and in therapy sessions than in their entire lives combined up to this point. The girls just want to know why, and so, everytime they think about Uncle Curt — calling him on FaceTime or over the phone, asking him for new toys or money for something mommy doesn't think they need; or even when the television happens to scroll across sports, the girls think about it too.

"I miss Uncle Curt." Olivia says somberly while dipping a nugget into sauce.

"Yeah, I do too." Elena seconds.

"Me too." Says Aunt Rach "We all do. But he still loves you all very much. And you'll see him again one day."

I slammed the bathroom door shut behind me, taking my place on the cold tile floor. I nestled my thighs between the toilet and the double vanity sink, and brought my legs close, bringing my knees to my nose, as if I meant to use them as an obstruction for a river of tears. I looked up momentarily, and saw the twinkle of the tub's faucet. My inner being wanted to scream, moving to another part of the house to let my heart further rot into confusion and angst, but I remembered the words San offered from my last therapy session.

"Some things will always bring back horrifying memories of that day, Eye. And we'll work slowly to identify those and develop some strategies for overcoming them. But, if you feel ready, there are some triggers we should slowly start to tear down, because you'll never get away from them."

I think the Chick-Fil-A is just one of those things that will always be there, that will always make me think of my brother. I suppose the bathtub is one of those triggers I simply have to confront.

Curt died in a bathtub. Of all the places he could've chosen to end his life, it was a tub. I think the confined space made him feel comfortable, at home in a way. He always told me his primary love language was touch, and towards the end of life, I don't think he was touched much. I think the tub gave him a sense of longing and love in a way. He didn't run the water. There was no music playing. He didn't leave a note. The television wasn't on. He had marginally cleaned up the bathroom, though it wasn't as deep as his normal bi-weekly scrub. He was fully clothed, dress neatly in his favorite, all-black Nike hoodie and black skinny jeans I had helped him pick out. He had on red and white Air Jordan 11's and a snapback representing his favorite basketball team, the Chicago Bulls.

I think he thought about it for quite some time, like he went back and forth about whether there was another way out, being meticulous about the current question at hand — whether he would take his own life or not. He was always methodical, a master strategist about everything, from his business to the women he dated to the day and time he decided to get his haircut every week. My brother never did anything without thinking about the consequences, good or bad. And in a way, that makes what he decided to do that much more frustrating. Like in my mind, I can see him, sitting down at the desk in his study, grabbing a sheet of paper, drawing a line down the middle, and writing on each side:

1. Reasons to live.

2. Reasons to not live.

I don't think he explicitly would write the word die.

I stare at the tub, grabbing a gob of tissue paper as I dry my face from the tears that have finally started to subdue. A few minutes later I bring myself to my feet, standing vertical once more, staring over the bathtub, empty and pearly white, as if freshly delievered and installed from Home Depot just hours earlier.

My sister, Rachel, has had the girls for the past few days. I would come visit, and occasionally spend the night, but Rach doesn't work, thanks to her husband's six-figure salary and her desire to be a stay-at-home wife. Just a few days after Curt's passing, I thought I had the strength to go back to full-time mommy mode. I had picked the girls up from school, and in the midst of prepping dinner, decided I would be efficient and simulateounsly do bath time. I cleaned the tub and turned the water on with little struggle, and then, just as I reached to lift Ilyana into tub, halfway full with warm water, I saw a glimpse of Curt's lifeless body flash before my eyes, a minature pool of blood so rich the soles on his shoes, once primer White, had become cherry red. I put Ilyana down by the tub, yelled for Olivia to finish bath time, and called Rach.

"I need you over here now, please."

I haven't been able to bathe my girls since, lest my mind flashback to his body; the gaping holes and wounds on each wrist; the box of blades in the window pane. The blood. My fuckin' god the blood. I can only imagine what it would've looked like, what he might have looked like, had he worn a color other than black. He ended up positioning his arms in a way that his hoodie soaked up most of it, but along the way, between cutting and drifting into the unknown, a not so insignifigant amount managed to flow at the basin.

What no one tells you about blood is that it doesn't stay all liquidy. It starts that way, but by the time the cops, fire department and EMT's come, invade your private space physically and emotionally, and wrap so much of your world onto a stretcher, it transforms into this clumpy mess. It's fuckin' impossible to get rid of. And no one tells you that you're responsible for cleaning it up, whether you hire someone or do it yourself. But what cleaning company comes in the middle of the night to clean up suicide blood?

It was a relatively mundane day. At the time, the hospital rotation had me on a ten week cycle, the one all the nurses dreaded. It meant you had Tuesday and Wednesday off for two months and some change. I took it in stride, knowing it only came around once a year or so. I got into a Tuesday routine, one that afforded me the luxury of getting all the girls ready for school without the pressure of getting to work on time. Once the caravan emptied, I treated myself to breakfast — Waffle House if I was feeling bubbly, Clyde's on Thompson St. downtown if I was feeling fancy. Then on to get my nails done before a midday nap and the afternoon bus driving session. Curt called the truck I drove a bus, because the girls would always pile in and out of it like the only thing missing was an automatic stop sign.

I still struggle. I haven't been to Waffle House or Clyde's since. My nails are ragged and bitten down and stale. I hate seeing school buses.

Tuesday. I fuckin' hate Tuesday's.

I pulled up to Curt's place after my nail appointment. Ironically enough, Tuesday was his self-proclaimed "off day" too, though Curt never really stopped working. I hadn't heard from him that morning, but figured he was tied up trying to get something done. We talked every morning, normally right after I dropped the girls at school but before his daily visit to the gym.

I parked my car in the usual visitors spot just a few steps away from his building, prancing onto the sidewalk and up the steps. Curt lived on the second floor, and I was all ready to ramble on about the shit my shift doctor pulled the other night, and the date I was considering ghosting the coming weekend.

I let myself in with my key and threw my purse on the kichen counter.

"Curt"! I yelled, expecting him to respond with his usual "Sup!" reply for greeting someone he geninely loves. The sup was usually followed by him running out of the bedroom with minimal clothing on.

His bedroom door was open, so I peaked in, seeing nothing out of the ordinary. The room wasn't clean but it wasn't dirty. Clean clothes spread everywhere, but no overflowing trash.

I've never seen or heard somone cry like this. To describe it as crying would be inaccruate. This isn't a cry. It's wailing, mixed with the sharpest sense of pain and grief I've ever felt palatable in my life.

I sat down next to my mother on her living room couch. I drape my right arm around her, using my left hand with a tissue in it to wipe the never ending stream of tears flowing from her face. Her baby boy was gone, and for a woman who prided herself on taking control of her happiness, this was a sense of grief she could do absolutely nothing about.

"What's the point of this"? I say emphatically while banging on the stereing wheel horn.

"I need to see it. I need to know." my mother said intently

"You think I'm making this shit up?"

"No, it's just…."

"It's just what!"

"I can't explain it, alright?" she roared back with an anger, one that I could see in her eyes was simply a cover up for the pain.

"I'm staying in the car."

My parents exited the vehicle, my father from the passenger side, coming to open the backdoor for my mother, like he has for 29 years. Their love – still so full, fluid and genuine. They've never been tested like this. When I get done thinking about taking my own life, I will be praying their marriage makes it through. I'm honestly not sure that any marriage can.

For the full 18 minutes my parents were in there, I just sat in the car, stoic. I haven't listened to the radio since the drive over to Curt's house earlier in the morning. I wondered what my parents were feeling. I shuttered to think the feeling that overtook my mother when they pulled that white sheet from his over face, and she finally had to accept the fact that he was really gone. The agony my father must feel, only to have to will himself to be a source of strength when he too needs someone to wrap their arms around him.

My eyes are still heavy, dreary like a towel that's been hanging to dry for a couple of hours. Even if I wanted to cry right now, I don't think I could. I must've emptied my ducts.

"What did I miss?" I ask myself repeatedly. "How in the world could *I* have missed this? Curt and I talked about *everything*. I knew he was struggling. I knew he was having a minor episode, but I've seen worse. *Much* worse. He didn't seem like he was anywhere close to *this*. He was just over at the house with the girls on Sunday, laughing and playing around, sneaking more cookies to them even after I said no."

"What the fuck happened, Curt? Why didn't you fuckin' call me?" I punch the steering wheel horn once more. I want to cry, but I don't have the energy.

My parents return to the car. No one says a word. I put it in reverse and drop them off back at home. My dad opens the car door for my mom.

"Wait one minute, baby girl." Dad says in a calm and reassuring voice.
"OK" I whisper.

Dad lets mom in the house. The window shades are open, allowing me to see directly into the living room. He takes her jacket and shoes off, placing them each by the table adjacent to the couch. Mom lays down, sinking her face into the pillow. My dad grabbed the comforter hanging over the back of the couch, covering up my mom.

The motion sent me into a tailspin.

It was not unlike the way the coroner's office covered Curt in the tub. I wasn't supposed to see that, but I slipped upstairs, partly in shock of what I had seen an hour ago, still not believing it was my baby brother in that bathtub. How could a gesture so terrifying in the morning be so soothing at night?

"We'll get through this, togehter." Dad said, ruffling his hand through my hair, using his big thumbs to wipe the tears flowing down my cheeks.

"You don't have to be strong for us, dad. You're allowed to hurt too."

"I know, baby." He said as he placed his palm over his eyes. He looked down at the gravel for what seemed like an eterniy. "But your mother needs me. You need me. Your brother… your brother was a good man. I'm proud of him and everything he accomplished. What an amazing life. I'm going to focus on that right now. I can grieve later."

He kissed me on my forehead and turned back to the direction of the front door.

"I love you, daddy."

"I love you too, pumpkin. You can stay here tonight if you'd like."

"I'm OK, dad. I'm OK. Promise." I said lying through my teeth.

"Let me know when you're home."

There are several bridges on the way home from my parent's house. One in particular is three lanes, hanging over a river. I thought about what it'd be like to just drive off of it one day. Right after Trenta was born, I suffered from really bad post-partum, to the point that on several occasions, I didn't want to live anymore. My saving grace in those moments was Curt. "If something happens to me, Curt will take care of the girls." I always thought to myself. I always knew that if I didn't come home one night, my children would definitely grieve, but I've never had any doubt about whether or not they'd be taken care of. Uncle Curt would spoil them, and then some.

I didn't realize how much of my life I discovered gone that morning. After my kids, Curt was my life. We were each other's life.

I drive over the bumpy steel plate connecting the roadway to the bridge. I stay in the middle of the three lanes, far enough from the water, to the point that any rash decision would at least take some mental work to ensure no one else is in the other lane.

I won't do it. I can't will myself to such. My parents would be devestated. My girls would lose their uncle and their mother in the same day. I want to die, but I don't have the courage to do it.

I pull back into my driveway. Rach must've left the downstairs lights on as she packed the girls up for an extended stay. I take my jacket off and throw it on the floor of the foyer. For the first time since I called my parents with the news, I look down at my phone.

23 missed calls.
63 unread text messages.

I throw my phone across the living room, hearing the cling as it tapped against the wall. I grab a comforter from the basket by the side of the couch. Putting an end to the worst day of my life. I truly hope I don't wake up.

"We want you to eulogize your brother." My mother said in a gentle tone.
"The fuck?"
"You two have always been inseperable" she said. "No one knew your brother the way you did. It makes sense for you to do it."

I got up hastily and grabbed a bottle of wine from the mini-cellar in the kitchen. I had decided to stay at my parents house for the next couple of days, at least until the funeral. The girls had stayed over here last night, but Rach took them once again, this time for a Friday full of pizza and board games. I filled the wine glass up to the rim and gulped half the glass before offering a response.

"Fuck it. OK."

"Language." My mother growled.

I fixated myself back onto the couch. Grandma Joy had made it into town last night, the first of an onslaught of family arriving in advance of the funeral. Curt and Grandma Joy were close. They talked at least once a week, and took an annual trip down to Costa Rica to visit the rest of our family that never made it to the States. Despite all of that, Grandma Joy lived up to her name during this time more than ever. She got up at the crack of dawn this morning and made everyone breakfast — platanos, rice and beans, sausage, potato cakes, fruit and coffee.

Curt was a coffee addict. I skip my cup this morning. I fuckin' hate coffee now, too.

The night before, she had stayed up with me, helping to walk me through the never ending onslaught of questions from the girls. They knew what had happened. Rach told them a version of it when she picked everyone up from school on Tuesday.

I held the girls tight Wednesday and Thursday night, sitting them down, explaining to them as best I could that Uncle Curt had gone to be with Jesus in heaven, and that they weren't going to get a chance to see him anymore, at least not on Earth. I wasn't even sure I believed the Jesus and heaven part, but it made them feel better. It made me feel better.

I picked Grandma Joy up from the airport, and she greeted me with a smile. I pulled over to help retrieve her bags. We hugged like we weren't entirely sure we would ever see one another again.

"I love you, grandma" I said, pulling back from the hug to gain enough distance to kiss her cheek.
"I love you, too."

The ride home was gentle and not as somber. I've never loss someone this close to me. I guess the initial pain stings to the point of being unbearable, and then the days between the passing and the funeral have an equal mix of emotions. I'm fairly certain I will never have a day in my life worse then last Tuesday, but I expect Saturday, almost 10 days after he died, to be a close second.

As we veered off the exit to my parents house, Grandma Joy broke a ten minute silence.

"You tell the girls?" She asks in her thick accent.
"Of course they know, grandma. What do you mean did I tell them?"
"No, no, child. Have you told them how he done it?"
"Not exactly." I said
"You have to tell them how he done it."
"Why?"
"You just have to. I can't explain it just listen to me."
"I don't know how" I offered. "Plus, they're not ready for that. That's a lot of shit. They just lost their uncle. That they know for a fact. That's enough for now.
"I'll help you tonight, OK." Grandma said as she pat my right shoulder from the passenger seat. "Are they asking questions?"
"Liv and Elena are, yeah. They know, the gist of it. They don't know how he did it. I haven't had the courage to share that. I ain't even tell them he killed himself. They're smart. They just kind of figued it out."
"They OK?"

"Liv isn't. She's been crying *a lot*. Can't get her to eat. Elena seems to just be blocking it out. Not happy or sad. I just…"

I take my glasses off and pinch my nose, trying to hold back the tears.

"It's OK." Grandma says, her words comforting in a way no one else's have been these past few days.

I got up from my seat in the front row, chewing the rest of my peppermint down to an easy point of swallowing. I looked up at the crowd of people. The sanctuary was packed. All of these folks were here, and they were all here because my baby brother touched them in some noticably special way.

I pulled my prepared notes from my pocket, and then shoved them back in.

"The world need not remember my brother for how his life ended." I started my speech.

"What happened?" Many of you asked in the days and weeks following my brother's suicide."

"I hate that question. I really fuckin' hate it. I have always hated that question."

"What happened?"

People would ask, both in-person and in comment sections on social media. Sometimes I held it together, saying generic things like "God called him home", or, "he was really struggling with depression", or, my personal favorite, "God doesn't make mistakes." Each time I typed one of those generic responses, my mind had a more unadulteraed, true to form version. "What the fuck do you think happened? He sliced both his wrist open and bleed to death in a bathtub on the second floor of his condo?"

I composed myself to deliver the rest of the eulogy with some semblance of restraint.

"I'm a keep it real with y'all — the circumstances around my brother's death are tragic. They fuckin' suck. They will *always* suck. They're heartbreaking. They leave me angry and bitter and confused and numb, all in the same day, and occasionally at the same time."

I tried to hold it together, tried to compose myself. I guess the moment was too much for even me to control. There I was, at the worst moment of my life, finally caving to a truth I was determined to ignore for my entire existence. I'm not always in control.

I let the tears flow, and they poured down my face like raindrops on the Mississippi. I stepped slightly down from the podium, just enough to grab the tissue paper on the table. I sniffled. I whispered to Curt, gesturing as I gazed over toward the coffin.

"I love you." I whispered, before finishing up what somehow proved to be the toughest two minutes of my life.

"I miss my brother… I miss him soooo fuckin' much." I giggled while wiping the snot from my cheeks.

"But… but yet, I've never been more angry at him. If he were to somehow get up out that coffin right now, the first thing I would do is punch him in his throat." I said jokingly, and for some strange reason, the crowd obliged in laughter.

"And then immediately after, I would hug him, hug him oh so tight, like I would never be able to do it again." I started wailing even more, multiplying the number of used tissues inside a new one I was picking up every five seconds.

"But hey, like I said, my brother need not be remembered for how his life ended, or even for that he ended his own life. That's not important, not so far as in his memory. If bringing back the piercing sorrow of his death is used to make sure that just one more person decides to live another day, then so be it. But please, I beg y'all, use it not for anything else."

I glaned over to the family section, noting the serene calmness of my dad and Grandma Joy. The still nature of mom. The mix of grief in the moment but pride in all Curt had done during his brief life.

"I think it's fitting that I was the one to discover Curt in the bathtub. Not playing around annoyingly with the girls. Not jumping up and down, screaming at the top of his lungs over some sports game. I was the one that saw him in that tub. Gone."

"But I was also the one that saw him the most, and saw him at the moments when he was most full of joy, most full of life. For me, for my family, for all of us, that's what we'll remember about Curt. The love and joy he showed us, even when we felt undeserving of it."

I started to put the microphone down. I didn't have much more to say, but then something dawned within me, as if Curt were there to counsel me through a painful part of my life once again, like he had done so many times before. I had gotten one step off the pulpit, but stepped back up to offer a closing.

"People that die by suicide are *more* than the final act. They are *more* than how they die. "

"My brother is more than his suicide. He is more than a depressive episode. He is more than his pain. He is twenty-six years of loving, gleeing, creative, ambitious life. I didn't deserve a brother like that. We didn't deserve a person like Curt. The world has been a worse place since last Tuesday, and I don't ever see life being any better than it was when I went to bed last Monday night. That's the kind of lover, fighter, brother Curt was. And you know what, I'm starting to realize, that's OK. If even just a handful of people know the world is a worse place whenever you leave it, hell, that's the sign of a life well lived."

I turned my body in the direction of the casket, to Curt's body, to deliver one final message.

"I love you, Curt. And I don't care how cliche it sounds or what people may think it to be — I will see you again, one day. Goodbye for now, little brother. I love you. Always and absolutely forever."

One More Light, Linkin Park
24

---

[24] White, Francis Anthony and Shinoda, Michael Kenji. "One More Light." *One More Light*, Warner Records Inc., 2017.

To the Lady at the Hippodrome Cafe that Used to Call Me Kendrick

My entire life
untitled and unmastered
Assumed to be a bastard
Tapping feet
like I'm happy feet
to please massa

But wait...

#

Those double doors like a token
Of my ever present evanescence
Your smile brings me to life

Like I got royalty inside my DNA
Like my pain has drifted away
Least for a millisecond
I'm stressin,
caressing shells
Wiping tears and recalling blessings
My lesson? Lecture at 7
My weapon? Class at 11

Depression is revvin

from my mind to this glock eleven

\#

But I choose to see the beauty
in the broken window pane
there's nuff pain for the both of us
And I come to realize that heaven
don't need no more despair
Less it's really like what them folks from ol'
down yonder say
Like dem Southern Baptist
then I reckon it ain't real
Or I ain't tryna be there no way
All the same

\#

I wanted to quit today
Not quit this here racist piece of shit
school
The one bearing the name
of the Black man they ain't let in
The one chiding me about papers,
free clinics,
FREE motherfuckin labor

As if my brother ain't wrapped in stray
healthcare ain't gone
Like I ain't rise at 5 to catch a train
back at 7
puncture and blister my ears

of notice and comment

Like I ain't get the note
bout the rent being due Tuesday
as if I get to comment bout this unlawful arrest
Mirandize these nuts
These walls where niggas study to fit robes
Sallie don't give no paper
make it safer for niggas on the roads —
Or even in her castle, to wit

Nah, I wanna leave it all
Burn the whole thing to the ground
And if a Tricky Dick goes limp as
The ashes crater,
So be it
Let that motherfucker burn

―――――

And that was only the last night. As in, my roller coaster of emotions from 10 to just now. But I would open those doors after crossing Baltimore & Paca. And it's like a Rodney King sized dumbbell had been lifted off my shoulders.

The power of a contagious smile.
Belief in my mind.
A whole buff chicken salad when I only had money for the half.
A free drink.

I was hungry. You fed me. I was thirsty. You gave me drink. Blessed are the meek.

I hope you inherit the Earth. And if not, I'm a take it and share a little piece with you.

Ann,

Please Mr. Postman, The Marvelettes[25]
Love, Kendrick Lamar feat. Zacari[26]

It's me, Fred.

I miss you.

I miss you a lot.

I wish you were here right now. I just need a hug. Nothing sexual or romantic or nothing like that. Just you, and your presence, and that smile, mixed with that one of a kind aurora you got that never fails to remind me life worth living another day.

But today, I'm really struggling. Like, staring out of windows and contemplating if I can make it through another winter, struggling. I don't want to die, but then again, I do. It's funny, maybe not literally, but funny nonetheless. What's a person to do when they're as sad and lonely as I am?

Did I mention that I miss you?

---

[25] Holland, Brian, Gorman, Freddie, Dobbins, Georgia, Bateman, Robert, Garrett, William. "Please Mr. Postman." *Please Mr. Postman*, Motown Records, 1961, 1991.
[26] Walton, Travis, Tiffith, Anthony, Kurstin, Greg, Duckworth, Kendrick, Spears, M., Pacaldo, Zacari. "Love." *DAMN.*, Aftermath/Interscope (Top Dawg Entertainment), 2017.

I honestly think I enjoy life. The chirping of the birds on a crisp Saturday morning. The sound of children playing. The scent of the most beautiful and feminine woman walking by with her sundress perfectly molded, her pedicured toes a utopian, bright summer color on a mid-July day. It was a canary, if I recall correctly. Such a mesmerizing glow off her melanin skin. The soothing nature of the rain. The oh so goregous rain, as winter turns to summer but gets stuck in-between what we used to call spring. There's a lot to live for, Ann. I'm just trying to find it … absent you.

I think I'm just fatigued, ya know? Not tired. Not sleepy. I think tired and sleepy are temporary statuses, truths and present feelings we're actually able to fulfill with solitude and rest. I need a year, maybe two; and a re-do of my childhood; and Ambien mixed with Zolar; and a hug. By God, do I need a hug. Do I need a hug from you. Your hugs, Ann. I need your hugs.

Sometimes I wish I could go back, but I don't know what I wish I would go back to. My heart and my mind feel elderly, again, and I'm so tired, like 78 years old at the end of my life that I've spent every part of me making sure those I love are taken care of, tired. Ain't no solutions for that. None except being close to you.

I miss you, Ann.

I miss you dearly. Will you come back to me? Can we talk about our lives and how fucked up things are to no fault of our own? Yet we keep fighting, battling through our inner loneliness and turmoil, and no one would ever guess how truly grieved our hearts are. No one truly understands.

Except you.

It's why I love you so much.

I Miss You, Beyoncé[27]

---

[27] Knowles, Beyoncé, Ocean, Frank, Taylor, Shea. "I Miss You." *4*, Columbia Records, 2011, 2012.

A Mother's Love

Daydreaming, Paramore[28]

I mean,
at its most basic level
it be like milds, from Harolds
Bout how many projects you think
gettin done this Chicago winter
only to question your existence
by early February

It's like clicking the mouse for the
fifty leventh time at 02:37
Reminiscing bout how naked women
soothed you as a kid for the first time
The day after 9/11
And you been looking for a Jada or
some fire to spark that same high ever since

It's like when you get that perfect chicken biscuit
The spicy kind
And you be thinking days later how good it was
How the chicken was pefectly thin
The biscuit immacutely buttered

---

[28] Williams, Hayley and York, Taylor. "Daydreaming." *Paramore*, Atlantic Recording Corporation, 2013.

The crisp and the warmth partioned
just right
So right that night before,
you set an alarm
Say you making it to this drive thru this AM
But Manuel ain't the chef on Saturday
And it wasn't so scrumptious this go round
And then that shit got discountinued

It's tongue kissing a razor blade
Gleaming out the window to bask into the shade
Yet changing your mind
Instead, I'll dot a little line on my thigh
Bout yay high
the blood off the blade glides
and it's a different high
Till you realize you wake up from this
And it becomes your go to, cheaper than
a therapist
In my feelings stead of in my bag
Not much in the way of a bag
But I cut a lot of lines
Besides, who's keeping score anyways

It's like the time you finally recognize the depths of your brainwashing.

Like yes sir no sir ain't no guarantee to get me home. And I don't dream of labor. Like the first few weeks when that new job don't feel like work, and er'body all giddy bout the new negra on payroll.

Reality ain't never too far behind
Just another grind
These niggas ain't shit
Like all the others
Like all the other niggas

It's like praying next to a butcher knife
slowly masquerading as a killer with a stroke
Smoother than Ray Allen in a South Beach corner
Wishing you were in a South Beach coma
Alongside a woman from South Beach named Mona
With a south beach moan
On the waves of a South Beach shore
Then having the door bust down like a
South Beach drug raid
Belt flying, as if your depression is some
meager excuse for attention
I was ready to die
And the only thing I was asked was what I got to be sad about?

It's like sitting in a parking lot with a would be friend
Them asking how you're doing
You,
for the first time in your life,
feeling safe, as if you're
in the presence of a person and a space where
you can be honest about your desire to
be no longer
Being honest
Open

Transparent
And finding that the desired reaction
was no more or less than
"I'm good, and you?"

I mean,
at its most basic level,
it's like Magic City.
Everyone knows the name,
but at the end of the night,
you'd be better off at Flame

Like Father, Like Son

Say I Didn't, Vic Mensa[29]

Life is this little nuanced mystery kind of jolting us along. We tend to naturally believe everything in front of our eyes. Sometimes it's true. Other times, it takes years of growth and maturity to reconcile falsehoods from reality.

I've been knocked down quite a few times. That's what life does, and I'm sure it isn't done putting me down. Yet each time, I've gotten up, dedicated, devoted and motivated to be better than I was last time. I learned all that and more from this man.

There are a lot of people that have taken credit for what I've accomplished in my life, and generally, I let them live. I don't feel the need to rain on other parades. But no one on Earth should ever feel more pride, more ownership, more accomplishment in anything positive I've ever done in my life than my father. He has quite literally always believed in me, and backed that belief up with whatever sacrifice was needed to help me get there.

He ain't perfect, he'll be the first to admit that, but the values I hold most dear to my heart - family, honor, sacrifice, faith, hardwork, accountability, love - those were instilled in me from an early age, and then reinforced over and over again by

---

[29] Baez, Alex, Lang, Carter, Garcia, Darian, Wilson, Ernest Dion, Tanner, John, Asher, Jordan, Jones, Malik Yusef, Griffin Jr., Tyrone William, Mensah, Victor, Pulliam, William Daron. "Say I Didn't." *The Autobiography*, Roc Nation Records, LLC, 2017.

him.

Flowers, man. Flowers are important, and we should all endeavor to give them to folks while they can smell them, and then pray we can give them more again and again and again.

I like to hit the town with my old man and make him feel young again, because he never fails to say how much he's proud of this tattooed son of his.

And those words are, without question, the best I could ever hear.

Love you, Pops.

<u>Depression Doesn't Win</u>

Note: I chose not to edit this because I have no desire to read it again. I wrote this in 2016, during a really tough time in life. I no longer identify with many of the sentiments expressed here, but I know there are quite a few people that might. So I've included it in this book in hopes of helping someone else. I'd like to see everyone get to a space of where I am now – full of life, love, gratitude and optimism. You are loved.

I've struggled with depressive moments for a while now. Some days/weeks/months are easier than others. Right now, I am fortunate enough to have learned a variety of ways throughout the years to help manage my depressive states. I am not writing this to be a hero. I am not. I am not writing this to be the first to speak so openly about such a prevalent problem, because I am not. Many people struggle with depression and anxiety. I am not special. I am not an anomaly. I am one of many.

I am writing this right now first and foremost for myself. I desperately need to be reminded of the tips, tools and structures I have put in place to help me manage. I am posting this out of hope that someone who often finds themselves in my shoes reads through these words, and that they find some level of motivation to keep fighting and keep living, even if it's only for today.

Now, I want to be amazingly clear here: depression is a disorder. People don't choose to be depressed, just like most people who take their own lives don't necessarily *choose* to commit suicide. There's something much deeper going on in the mind, heart, brain, body and spirit that can't be explained with a Facebook status or tweet. On top of that, depression is not merely an attack from Satan. I do not in any manner believe that prayer and scripture reading are the only answers to depression.

Let me clarify: I believe in the power of prayer and the Holy Spirit to rid me of my depression as much as I believe in that same power to start my business. No, I cannot start and run a successful business without the hand of God, but I also can't sit on the couch, eat cereal and play FIFA all day either. There's a balance, and it's one that includes spiritual and practical means of management and pursuit. This post is mostly aimed at the practical side, but I do mention the role that Christ has played in management over the past few years.

As a child, there were days when I would do nothing but sit in my room and stare out the window. Occasionally, in between looking out at the passing cars and the skies, I would scribble down notes in my journal. Some of those notes would be morbid, other notes were laden with profanity, and sometimes I would write about sports. I would look, and I would write. That's all I could muster up the emotional energy for. I first thought about killing myself when I was ten years old. The details of this occasion are outlined in my book (*A Memoir: on Love & Life*) so I won't go into detail about this. From it, I learned how to talk through my emotions and process my anger. I found different techniques to help me through my times of loneliness. I discovered a myriad of ways to continue to motivate myself, even when a part of me felt like I didn't want to live.

People who don't struggle with depression can have a hard time relating to it or understanding it. Let me assure you: few individuals who are actually struggling with depression want you to know they go through it. We already feel alone, weak and vulnerable, and the last thing we want to do is invite someone into our space that doesn't have the slightest idea what we're going through or how we're feeling.

I would sit in the middle of my room in the middle of the night, sobbing, asking myself "Why am I sad? Why do I want to die?" As time went on and I learned more, it became more apparent to me: being sad for "no reason" is a part of having depression.

Granted, there are times when some of my more vulnerable moments are brought on because of school, work, family or stress. But there are countless other times when things in life seem to be good, and yet, and I would think to myself: Lord, I will not take my own life, but if for some reason I die right now, I will not be upset.

That's merely a backdrop. I can't give you an entire understanding of what it's like to deal with this, because I honestly believe I could put that in a book. Hopefully what I have offered suffices. Now, how do I manage it?

For starters, my depression is a direct explanation of why I love so hard. You take that how you wish. It's why it hurts when people I haven't seen in a while can't find anything else to say to me but "hey stranger." As if our cell phones don't work both ways, and as if I didn't call you a few weeks ago, you picked up and told me you had to call me back, and never did. I don't mind it, you have a life to live, but please refrain from calling me a bad friend in so many ways. I resent that. I strive to be a great friend because loving hard is one way I manage. I try to turn pain and heartache into substance for loving, so when I offer that love, and it isn't reciprocated even half way, it hurts, and it cuts rather deeply.

Another way I manage is through exercise. During my high school years, I didn't struggle much because football was such an amazing outlet. It gave me the physical contact I needed. It gave me friends. It gave me a goal and objective to strive and live for each day. It was a saving grace. When that got taken away, I didn't know what to do for a while. I joined a lot of clubs and organizations during college, but those were more self-medicating activities than anything else. The first year of law school was one of the toughest years of my life, and I did a poor job of managing. I was often intoxicated from Thursday night until Sunday morning, just in time to watch football all day. It worked for me, at least I thought: I was entrenched in school work from Monday until Thursday evening, intoxicated from

Thursday evening until Sunday morning, and lived my life through football players on Sunday. It seemed like a good strategy, until it wasn't. I eventually got back in church, but I also started lifting weights and running miles again. This was a godsend.

I don't know the science behind exercise or what it does to your brain, but it has been monumental in giving me something to consistently look forward to; something to challenge myself. I'll often run four or five miles a day and pretend I'm playing for Arsenal in a London Derby. Is it weird? Maybe. Does it work for me? Absolutely. It not only gives me more energy and puts me in a better mood, but it's something to help channel my energy into. If I'm sad, I'll run it out. If I'm angry, I'll take it out on the barbell.

When managing, it's also important to keep close with the ones you love. I went back to seeing a therapist, and she encouraged me to do a lot of things, the main one being go home to Atlanta more often. If you know, I love my family. Nothing else matters more. Not being around them for extended periods of time can be frustrating and saddening. I don't want anyone feeling like they have to walk on egg shells around me or be on their best behavior, because all that will do is tick me off. I'm still a man, an imperfect man at that, and all of life's ills cannot be attributed to depression. My family and friends get that. They know when I'm just being a jerk and need to be corrected, but they also know when I'm going through a tough time. It's not something I can really coach anyone up on, all I can really do is let you know about the struggle, and pray you extend me grace as we learn and work through things together.

One other key way I manage is through my faith, which can be tricky sometimes. I like to consider myself an intellectual, and one of the things I do *too* much of when I am down is think. Sometimes I'll think that I'd be better off if there were no God, because then all of life's ills are simply the product of luck, a mere probability.

Whenever I think like this, I am quickly snapped back to reality. I believe in an afterlife. I believe in the redemptive power of the blood of Jesus Christ, and that belief helps pull me out the dun drums. It's like God demonstrates his love for us in that while we were yet sinners, Christ died for us. (Romans 5:8). Christ died for me: knowing I would curse out people who cut me off; knowing I would be prideful, jealous and enviousness. That's a pretty huge deal. I hold onto that, and I hold on to the all encompassing feeling of love, freedom and redemption I have in Jesus, and then I am even more motivated to want to live happily and freely, all in an effort to tell other people about this Jesus.

This post is long enough. If you're going through the struggle, know that you're not alone. I'm here, whenever you may need someone. I love you.

Summer 2020

Summer 2020 - interlude, Jhene Aiko[30]

I cannot let go...

Of memories destined to be created
dreams fulfilled
promises kept
Love
And the love we never made

I've been missing you...

Not just for 10,000 hours
but for eternity
and I think
Of the finite time we have
the vapor of summer
Of this summer
Of the summers we get on earth
of the summers we have to bask in this endless stream of care
I can't let go
not only of you
that feeling

---

[30] Chilombo, Jhené Aiko Efuru and Viet Le, Julian-Quan. "Summer 2020 - interlude." *Chilombo*, Def Jam Recordings, 2020.

the lil pit in my stomach
confronting the truth
that I only have you
Now
And then 10,000 years
And then forever more
And I'm honestly not too sure
I even want that

Sometimes I cry...

Thinkin bout the day Stevie died
of all the people I've said
A final goodbye to
Already
And I don't even know it yet
I mean,

It feels good to be alive...

To whine
in the dancehall
with your lips and your hips
And your lips
on mine
sweat glistening your spine
Drissling onto my
Essence
As we caress one another
Creating our own dance floor
with not a care in the world
till you start that lil finger twirl
from my neck

to the muscular part of my back
maybe that's why they call em traps?
Bodies intertwined
sundress sticking to skin
It's our time
We play Skin in the background,
fresh wax under your Fenty nightgown
Murder in the first degree
I know you really love me
Whatever comes of this night,
shall be
We mutually bypass the rubbers
consider that our consent decree

And there's not a doubt in my mind…

we were meant to be together
Maybe not forever.
Maybe so.
But these moments
preordained
And they were slain
And that's definitely the worst

That your still here, right here, by my side…

Even on the other end of an empty bed
I still think about you
The drag of dry humor
Your giggle from all the puns intended
Your moan right before you ended
The scent you left
Not only the t-shirt I fetched from

besides the shoe box on the back shelf in the closest
But the fragrance you left on my soul
It'll never go away
There's a part of you that'll forever stay
And that's OK

I'll take some rain with my sunshine

Alex Palace

23 years ago, my little brother was born.

My world changed forever.

There's so much we've been through, he and I individually, together, and as a family, that I want to reconcile. Sometimes I think that will happen. Other times I think not. I'm learning not everything in life comes with an explanation or finality, and that's OK. Ambiguity can breed imagination.

My brother is one of the millions of young adults in this world with Autism Spectrum Disorder, or ASD. We are fortunate. My brother can have conversations, bathe and feed himself, and enjoy many things this life has to offer. We frequent Atlanta Braves games and visit his favorite restaraunts, Olive Garden and Carabba's. We talk about the scores from the sports games, and he can tell you the "Baltimore Orioles suck." He has his cell phone, and often calls to let me know that his day went well, that he cleaned the windows at work, and that he's excited for Friday night so he can get his quesadilla from our favorite Mexican restaurant. Since I moved out of state, he can tell me he misses me, he can understand that I miss him, and we can count down the days until we are united.

Through my experience navigating the world and helping to raise him, I found many other individuals with ASD that can't do many of those things I mentioned. Some can't feed themselves. Some are confined to a wheelchair and will never know what it means to walk in the park, run the bases at SunTrust Park, or play catch in the yard with their big brother. They'll never feel the joy or experience of gathering in the kitchen with a loved one and helping to chop the onions or roll the pasta for a family meal that may be low on eloquence but high on love. It doesn't mean their lives are any less fulfilling, but it soothes my sometimes-weary soul to know that at least some of the things I dreamed of doing with my little brother are able to come true.

Having a loved one with special needs or disabilities is a calling. It tests and perfects you in ways nearly nothing else can. It is often said that those of us called to love those with intellectual disabilities often mourn that which could have been, that should have been. I don't think a truer sentiment has ever been spoken.

Through growth and maturation, therapy and introspection, I have learned to appreciate part of this as reality. Nevertheless, I have also learned that grief is OK, that's there no moment of acceptance, and that reconciling the nuanced emotions of being deeply connected with and loving someone with an intellectual disability never disappears. In a way, it's like continuously mourning. There's a loss that took place when that diagnosis was given. There's no closure. No acceptance. No point where it no longer affects you. Like every loss in life, there are good days, and there are not so good days. Through it all, you love them. Through it all, you power thorugh.

I love my brother exponentially. I care about him more than anything else in the world. There is literally nothing I would not do for him. I love him wholeheartedly for who he is now, and I am not ashamed of that. I also mourn what could have been on a daily basis. I mourn that we've never played 2K together, that I can't fly out to whereever he is attending college and spend a night or two with him, that I can't call and vent to him about work or my relationship. All of these feelings are valid, and they don't diminish the love I have for him.

My brother changed my life for the better. I owe much of who and what I am today to him, his unconditional love, and his existence here on this earth. In a way, I have found that many of my needs, my areas of imperfection and shame, have been revealed, sharpened and healed through him. I am forever grateful for that.

Here's to 23 years, Alex. I pray to God daily for many many more.

Birthday Thoughts/Forward

Born Tired, Jhené Aiko[31]

Today, I get to celebrate another year of life, and while I have never been much of a celebratory birthday person, I'm starting to change as I get older. Every birthday is worth commemorating, because I never know if I'll get another one.

This song perfectly encapsulates where many of us are right now. When I first heard it, I was in North Carolina for work. I was driving on 40-W and had to pull over because I couldn't control my sobbing. I hadn't cried in YEARS. Growing up it was because toxic masculinity told me men didn't cry. Recently, I've just poured my emotional energy into work. But those few minutes literally took so much pain, anger and stress off my shoulders. I put the car back into drive and headed to my meeting. I felt heard, validated and understood. Such is the power of art.

I know some of our feelings have gone from anger, outrage and energetic to depressive, exhausted and hopeless. You are not alone, and your feelings, no matter where they are on the spectrum, are valid. The moral arc of the universe is long, but it bends toward justice. While we can make very real and impactful change immediately, the reality is our full fight for a more moral and just society is a lifetime's work. It's a marathon, not a sprint, and the marathon must always continue.

---

[31] Warfield, Brian Keith, Chilombo, Jhené Aiko Efuru, Robinson, Maclean. "Born Tired." *Chilombo*, Def Jam Recordings, 2020.

So I'm thankful for the birthday wishes in advance. I know a lot of people that never made it to this point, and to be honest, I shouldn't have either. But in my lowest moments, the Lord graciously sent reminders, sent comforters and people to show an unwavering amount of love and appreciation. When I didn't believe I was enough, God reminded me that I am. I was reminded via family and friends; via various art forms; via my imagination; via hope in what the future holds.

I suppose my exaltation for today, tomorrow and indefinitely is to prioritize your own well-being. Take care of your mental. Many of us, as Jhené notes, have been fighting our entire lives. From micro-aggressions at work; to being passed over for opportunities you're more than qualified for; to not having any recourse or validation for sexual harassment or abuse; to doing your darnest to raise change agents that give back to the world and then some; to pulling to the side of the road for a traffic stop, genuinely believing your life is about to be over.

Life is hard, but there are moments that are so glorious. In times like these, you have to work to find and create them. Maybe now more than ever, we need to make that endeavor. So I pray everyone find time and space to step back from the work, to heal and re-center themselves, and spend time with the ones you love. If there's someone in your life that deserves flowers you haven't yet given them, make it a priority to do that. Let's love one another while we're here instead of regretting what we didn't do when they're gone.

> *"Rest your weary heart*
> *Dry your teary eyes*
> *I know you are scarred*
> *And torn a part inside…"*

Darling, so am I…

If you identify with those words and ever need encouragement, I'm here for you. Be kind to yourself. You are not worthless. You are not a failure. You are worthy of love. You are worthy of life.

Love, Jhené Aiko
32

---

[32] Warfield, Brian Keith, Chilombo, Jhené Aiko Efuru, Viet Le, Julian-Quan, Robinson, Maclean. "LOVE." *Chilombo*, Def Jam Recordings, 2020.

Open Letter to Eternity

Hi, God:

It's me, Fred. How's it going up there?

I'm doing aight, God. Really good, actually. Haven't cut myself in ages. And my brother's doing really great. Even workin a lil job na. He says he cleans tables and such. In fact, he say that's all he do. But I know it's way more than that. It's just I usually talk to him at the end of the day, when he's ready to relax and watch sports, so cleaning tables it is.

God, even though things are good, I be wondering if you remember me? Like, if you think about me? Like I be thinkin it's impossible, like a such a Big ol' God can be thinkin bout all the peoples in da world and still have time for lil ol' me. How that work, God? How you be all in the same places at the same time? Hearin all dem prayers and stuff?

I be in my bed alone at night, God, thinkin bout life, tryna envision what heaven goin be like. And I ain't even goin lie, I be gettin up tight sometimes, with a lil pit in my stomach and butterflies floatin round, cos I be thinkin I might get weary of singing your praises, ya know, shouting holy holy for the rest time and stuff. It ain't that I don't love you, I do, shoot, I can't wait to see you. Bow before you. See Grandma Kat and Grandpa Rudy, Granny, Tupac, Jack Kennedy and all dem.

Oh, and Zora – by god I gotta meet Zora.

But God, can you do me a favor? Can you send me a lil nudge every once and a while down here, ya know, remind me that you reals and all?

And it ain't gotta be a separate heaven for G's, but is it mountains? Can you make some mountains up dere? Like scenic ones, with greenery and trails to hike in the fall? And slopes in the winter? And a view of some water?

And just a couple notebooks laying around on blankets? Oh, and music, like in headphones and stuff, just that neo-soul from lovely women in the UK.

I like that, God. It soothes my spirit.

Acknowledgments

I have so many incredible people in my life, and I'm glad I stuck around long enough to be able to appreciate y'all.

Thank you so much to all of my family and friends. You know who are, and you should take some pride in this work of art. I will refrain from attempting to list names because there are simply too many.

My dad has always uniquely encouraged me to chase my dreams and be creative, no matter how weird or far-fetched what I want may sound. Thank you for always believing in me.

Tric, you take my random calls at all times of the night and send me random Jhené Aiko videos, and they are always so timely. You are my rock. I love you. Yolanda, you're always down for a good meal after we argue about something. It's carthartic. Thank you. Alex, you are simply the best. I love you all.

Kelly Dawsey met me at a Taco Mac in Kennesaw, Georgia one December night, and believed in this vision for a creative arts company. We got a long way to go, but thanks for believing in me, bro. Hope I don't let you down.

My Aunt Dee has been my biggest writing cheerleader for as long as I can remember, and my Aunt Janet helped me have a comfortable space to explore my creativity in piece.

Last but certainly not least, thank you to my wonderful partner, Brandi. Thanks for being my partner and crime, for letting me walk around and randomly recite scenes from movies, and to disappear into the office for days at a time trying to spark something out of nothing. Much of what is discussed in these pages prepared me to know how to love you well. I am thankful for those experiences. I am thankful for you.

Thank you, Lord.

About Relentless Love

Relentless Love is a media and creative arts company devoted to producing quality and thought-provoking art focused on sports, politics, pop culture, art and more.

Relentless Love's chief objective centers around producing quality content via writing, videos, books, merchandise and podcasts. Over time, those artistic offerings will be further complemented by short stories, novels, plays, short films, and, eventually, feature length films. We hope you'll join us on our journey as we strive to be relentless. To further support our work, please visit us at www.relentless.love, follow us on social media, join our email list, and share our content with family, friends and colleagues.

We're a small start-up company, and that means we don't yet have the resources of some larger groups. As a result, you may have noticed some errors in this book. Most books undergo almost a dozen edits, but because of budget restraints, we could only manage a few. If you notice errors, please be kind in sending an email to info@relentless.love so we can edit those out of future prints.

About the Author

F.E. Curtis, II is a writer, strategist and activist. He is the founder of CTK Strategies, a public affairs consulting firm, and Relentless Love, a media and creative arts company. He is also the author of *A Memoir: on Love and Life* and host of several podcasts. (All 22 Podcast, The Base, Politics As Usual and The Journey) He is a citizen of the world, but his things are in Virginia and Georgia.